the SELL PROCESS

A simple yet profound process to help *anyone* and *everyone* sell skillfully

by: **Don Buttrey**

The SELL Process™
Published by Sales Professional Training, Inc.
Beavercreek, Ohio 45434
www.salesprofessionaltraining.com

Book cover by Ryan Buttrey.

Printed in the United States of America by BookMasters, Inc.
(2nd Edition)

Library of Congress Cataloging-in-Publication Data:

Buttrey, Donald Paul
 The SELL Process / Don Buttrey
ISBN-10 0983907307
ISBN-13 978-0-9839073-0-5
1. Selling.   2. Sales Management.   3. Sales Coaching.
4. Communication. I. Title

Contents

Introduction

This book was written to help anyone and everyone sell skillfully. If you have an objective with another person, the simple process offered in this book provides the framework to prepare and execute that interaction. As you read this book, you can initially apply the process by starting with an actual selling interaction that you are facing—or will face. As I walk you through each step of the SELL Process, you will discover that it can become your personal tool to help you get results and action with other people.

The sales profession encompasses a wide array of activities. It can demand a host of skills, disciplines, duties, and strategies—often unique to the particular industry or market served. As a sales trainer, I am aware of this broad spectrum. Nevertheless, there is one integral component that is critical to all selling activity. All selling involves dynamic interaction between people. Tactical selling—the actual interaction with customers—is where sales are won or lost.

Mastering the SELL Process is a must for career sales professionals. From territory sales, to telesales, to retail—it all involves interaction. Sadly, many salespeople have been trained in product, application, presentation, territory, etc.—yet so few have received training in the *process* of selling.

For those readers who are not necessarily in a sales career, the SELL Process can also equip you. You may have noticed that many of your everyday interactions with people are actually *selling* interactions.

Many books start with a dedication. Granted, I have many individuals to thank that have helped make this book a reality. However, what drove me to expound on this process in writing was the notable selling improvement it produced in salespeople as I trained and coached them over the past two decades. Once they began to apply the SELL Process to tough selling situations, I would see the lights come on and wheels start turning in their heads. (I love what I do!) After thousands of trainees responded consistently with sustainable selling improvement, I knew it was time to share this empowering process with a broader audience.

This book is dedicated to *you*, no matter what your particular calling or lot might be. Let's learn and apply the SELL Process!

Chapter 1
The SELL Process

We all sell

Think about the times when *you* engage in the role of selling. We all sell.

We all sell in many aspects of everyday life. Nearly all of us have sold our ideas or opinions to others. Often, we are *selling* to our spouse, siblings, even our children. At times we may *sell* action or changes to an employee, colleague, or boss. Non-profits and charities *sell* their vision to solicit donations and support. Professional territory salespeople and those who *sell* on the phone need to grow their business and secure orders. Business owners and CEOs *sell* to potential investors the capability of their organization to produce revenue and profitable returns. Engineers and designers *sell* the feasibility of their new designs or solutions.

Red Motley observed, "Nothing happens . . . until somebody sells something."

When people are faced with the need to sell a product, idea, or an action, I have found that most are uncomfortable with the activity. They don't know where to start or how to assure success. It seems that the majority of people are quick to confess, "I am not a salesperson." Some admit that they do not want to be. When faced with a challenge to interact with another person, having a specific objective in mind, the apprehension can feel unnerving.

Even career salespeople can be dismayed by the task of actual selling! Many lean on their ability to present or articulate and never grasp what *selling* really is—becoming satisfied with merely an enthusiastic presentation of products, services, or applications. Many dread prospecting and cold calls. They avoid proactive selling and primarily respond to quote requests, visiting mostly customers and contacts that like them—becoming what I call "professional visitors." This might lead to a tendency to spend time providing service or support and *not* selling. Many flounder in tough negotiation encounters.

These interactions, in which we all do this thing called selling, subject us to the risk of rejection, avoidance, or misunderstanding. Reaching our objective is uncertain and we feel a lack of control. Some selling interactions make us feel like we are pressuring or begging the other person. And all of the misconceptions and misunderstandings about selling loom in our minds. What is selling? Why do people fear it? Is it a gift of ability that some personalities are just born with?

There are so many books on selling and yet the process and application still seem to evade the masses. That is why this simple, yet profound, book had to be written.

What is selling?

At first thought, most would say that selling is peddling products or services. For some, selling might actually conjure up negative thoughts or images of slick talking, manipulative "blow-guts" or the classic door-to-door salesperson. Others may think that selling is what people who have outgoing or assertive personalities can do to make a living.

Many have taught that selling is simply about finding a need and meeting it. Granted, there is much truth to the philosophy that selling is fulfilling needs. Consultative selling is credible and has the right focus the customer, the other person. Still, there are cases where the customer or other person doesn't know or understand what they need. They must be persuaded that another course of action is to their benefit.

Does this lead to the conclusion that selling should be defined as negotiation power and persuasiveness? Is selling the task of effectively presenting your solution and getting the desired response or action? It does seem that much selling is simply getting other people to want to do, and to do, what you want them to do. Is it all about not taking no for an answer? Perhaps then, the key would be persistence.

Maybe it is the skill of building relationships. Selling is all about people and networking. Therefore, it might be logical to conclude that selling is about being likable and friendly to people.

Some say that selling is strategic—getting in the right market, getting in front of the right people, going to the top decision makers. This school of thought promotes the idea that selling is finding the right buyer—to qualify and close, or move on to the next potential opportunity.

There are those who define selling as being able to effectively communicate your value, proving that what you have or offer is clearly better.

These are some of the conclusions reached about selling that can all be true in a myriad of situations. All true, yet many of these philosophies, or methods of selling, can be unsuitable in given situations. And selling becomes elusive, overwhelming and perplexing.

Let me help all the readers of this book by providing a fundamental understanding about selling:

Selling is a PROCESS.

Selling is a process

Selling is simply a process of interaction for mutual benefit. The applications for each reader as you learn this simple, yet profound, process will be far-reaching. If you can grasp this process that I will show you, and learn to apply it in *your* selling situations, you can be effective at selling!

This book is for *you*. For everyone who wishes for that ability to sell effectively as a professional or in those everyday situations—this handbook is designed to lift the haze and provide clear understanding. I will not tell you what to say. I will not suggest goofy or corny things to do. No tricks. No manipulation. No complicated, abstract model of selling. No clever, new sales techniques. Just solid help on how to perfect each unique interaction with the other person. Understanding the process will empower you to figure out what to say and how to respond. The SELL Process will provide a framework so that you can prepare and execute highly effective selling. My service to you in this writing will not be to meticulously apply the process to specific selling applications. The spectrum of application is exhaustive! I will simply present the SELL Process in a clear way so that you can embrace it and unleash its power in every interaction that you face.

The SELL Process is foundational. All the wisdom and insights from a thousand books on selling can be integrated into your utilization of the SELL Process. Once you recognize this, everything you have learned about communication, people, interviewing, psychology, value-selling, motivation, negotiation, etc. can be harnessed, as you prepare and execute effective interaction with the SELL Process. You can master the SELL Process!

For sales professionals, those who have chosen a career in sales, the SELL Process is absolutely essential! The profession of selling is a high calling that demands a wealth of understanding and specific application for each unique market, organization, competitive position, and aspiration. Selling is a skillful art that requires years of development and practice. My life's work is dedicated to intensive training to help these professionals perfect their selling. At the very heart of the broad spectrum of everything I teach to sales professionals is the SELL Process. For individuals, the challenge of effective, specific application will come with a regimen of disciplined usage of the SELL Process— with purposeful improvement.

For organizations, the application and reinforcement

will occur in training camps, sales meetings, and ongoing coaching. Standardizing this versatile tool into your entire organization has boundless benefits.

Before I unfold the SELL Process and give you detailed help on how to apply it in your world, let's shed light on some basics about selling in general.

First, it is important to clarify that selling always has a focus or objective. Selling is not merely discussion. Much selling activity is proactive; the seller has a defined objective, or a set of objectives, to accomplish with the other person. This is imperative for professional salespeople. If *you* don't know what you are trying to do, the customer certainly doesn't! A clear, action-oriented objective is also a must for *any* selling interaction. But, please understand, the SELL Process must not be strictly about you. Ultimately, the focus must be on the other person, the customer, the buyer. Their needs and wants are the target. You must confirm suspected needs and uncover wants. You must identify their perceptions or perhaps learn how to effectively change perceptions in an effort to satisfy the other person and create a both-win outcome. Unfortunately, our human nature is fixated on self-focus. Thus, the need is evident for a process that can help us do assertive selling, while maintaining a consultative, sincere focus on the other person.

The next basic tenet is that selling is essentially interaction. I love that particular word: interaction. What is the last part of that word? *Action.* And if you want to get action, action on your objective, or action on the next logical step with someone—you must become a master of the interaction. Selling is not simply a monologue, a pitch, or a presentation. By all means it is not the proverbial "dog-and-pony-show." Selling is a dialog involving communication and human behavior. Selling is all about relationships. With that said, in conjunction with the SELL Process, there is a lifetime of continuous improvement ahead for each of us to get better at relationship skills and disciplines. The SELL Process, with daily application and critique, will become a structure to help you apply and implement lessons learned throughout your career and life. It should be noted that when I train sales professionals, significant training emphasis is spent on communication skills, listening disciplines, and adapting to all styles of people. You will see that the process facilitates application and integration of all the essential components of relationship selling.

Conclusively, selling is undeniably a **process**. Accepting that simple principle and building on it empowers you to sell! You see, the process provides a systematic and logical control of the dynamic interaction.

Read that sentence again. Let it sink in.

This appears to be an oxymoron—systematic and logical *control* . . . of a *dynamic* interaction, (that could go in any direction during diverse responses from idiosyncratic human beings). But yes, the SELL process does give you control! It is not a cure-all and will surely not prevent the free choices of the person you are interacting with–but it is logical and organized, helping you to maximize every situation and opportunity. After teaching the SELL Process in a recent seminar, one individual approached me after the training and exclaimed: "I was lost, but now I'm found!" As he finally learned and began to understand the process of selling, he was empowered.

The customer or buyer process

Now that we have established the premise of the SELL process, it is obvious that there is also a process that the other person goes through—a customer or buyer process.

In order to satisfy needs and wants, customers qualify and consider goods and services from vendors. In interaction with a salesperson, customers go through a customer process. In a similar fashion, anyone who is faced with a decision to acquire something, make a choice, or take an action, will go through some semblance of a process. The center of their target, so to speak, is to take some action that will meet their perceived needs and wants.

This process, is of course, dynamic and can be convoluted. It may not always be step-by-step. The important thing to acknowledge is that it is logical—and it is in tandem with the SELL Process.

To help visualize this initially, I will provide a target model.

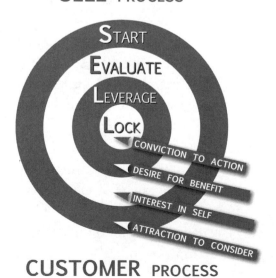

SELL PROCESS

START
EVALUATE
LEVERAGE
LOCK

CONVICTION TO ACTION
DESIRE FOR BENEFIT
INTEREST IN SELF
ATTRACTION TO CONSIDER

CUSTOMER PROCESS

The customer (or buyer) process begins with an **attraction to consider.** This can begin from an idea one gets, advertisements or marketing, suggestions from others, or a proactive approach initiated by a seller. Something begins the process. No one is going to buy anything if they don't know it is there. There will be no action if the buyer is not first attracted somehow to the need to act.

From there, the customer or buyer considers or investigates, and is at the very heart of the matter, concerned with **interest in self**. Chances are high that people are not thinking about you or what you want. Their preoccupation is focused on what they might gain from getting or doing the thing at hand. Once they see something of interest, once they see something that they might want . . .

. . . a **desire for benefit** occurs. What drives action, and what motivates people to spend money is when they perceive how they could possibly benefit. If that desire becomes strong enough for them; if they can get past any hindrances or limitations . . .

. . . they will reach the center of their target–a **conviction to action**. Conviction is a compelling characteristic. Typically, when people buy something or take action it is because they are convicted in their mind to do such a thing. Often, they will defend or recommend the action to others! It amazes me how people who buy a certain product or brand want to herald their action by wearing a hat or displaying a memento. Have you ever seen a pick-up truck with a sticker on the back window, proudly condemning a different brand? It seems to be a true statement that *people love to buy.* And when they buy, it is because they were convicted internally to take the action. They went through their buyer process and happily reached the center of the target. So, they are not adverse to the process, per se, but seller, take heed. People may love to buy–but they hate to be sold!

It is pivotal to respect the process that the other person is going through! Our challenge, as sellers, is to be alert and intuitive in recognizing where the other person is in the process, and help them to the center of the target. This is where our process, the SELL Process, comes into tandem play. Based on our preparation of the SELL Process and our practiced ability to adapt to the dynamics, we keep the process in harmony.

The **SELL** Process is:

Start—to attract
Evaluate—to discover interests
Leverage—to match discovered desires with Benefits
Lock—to confirm conviction and agree to action

Here is an important assertion about the activity of selling, which is the crux of the process concept. Selling, as defined earlier, is interaction for mutual benefit. Based on this premise, you cannot *make* someone buy from you or take action. They must be internally convicted and thus take action. The SELL Process, our side of the target progression, is designed to help us both get to the center of the target *together*. The use of trickery or manipulation is short-term and will backfire, often destroying the relationship and continued business together. Using only power or persuasiveness leads to fear, skepticism, and buyer's remorse.

Remember the old saying, "You can lead a horse to water, but you can't make him drink?". Well, it is true, and applicable here. But let's add one more phrase to that saying. You can lead a horse to water, but you can't make him drink—*but you can add salt to his oats.*

The processes are like a dance. Not a vaudeville show dance, but a relationship slow dance in which the customer/ other person is in the lead. I wish I was in the lead, but that is not the case in true consultative selling. I have an objective, and by skillful interaction with respect and keen awareness, I orchestrate the maximum both-win outcome. Then the action taken is essentially "their idea."

Keeping the process in harmony and getting to the center of the target successfully is not only possible; it is the prize of learning and mastering the SELL Process! As you will discover on our journey through this book, your success rate is not guaranteed. However, the process will help you maximize your effectiveness and utilize the elements of control that you *do* possess. You will see how helpful strategy, awareness, listening, flexibility, relational skills, and a sincere focus on the other person become, as you interact and navigate the SELL process to the center of the target! Your preparation before the interaction is your investment to ensure success.

Chapter 2
SELL Offense: preparation before the interaction

Selling interaction can be greatly improved as you learn to utilize the SELL Process. The framework, S-E-L-L, becomes a tool that can be used to prepare before a pending interaction or sales call. This could be compared to preparing your offense before you go into a game situation. You will also discover that this same SELL Process can be used as a framework and methodology to prepare for defensive situations. In dynamic selling interactions the other person could put you on the defense in a moment's notice. The functionality of the SELL Process is that it helps you prepare for both offense and defense! This simple, but profound process can be utilized to prepare your *offense* before specific interactions and to prepare *defense* for typical or expected objections, complaints, or negotiation ploys! One tool—to prepare for winning offense and defense.

Coach Bobby Knight said, "The will to win is not nearly as important as the will to prepare to win." It has also been said that failing to plan is planning to fail. These truisms apply significantly to the SELL Process. Interaction with another individual, whether in front of the person or on the phone, is where sales and results happen. Every interaction or sales call counts, and when you have those precious interactions you must maximize them and get incremental action!

Be careful not to fall prey to the excuse, "You never know what will happen in a dynamic interaction so why prepare?" I will admit that anything could happen. However, I have discovered over and over through my many years of selling experience, that appropriate preparation using the SELL Process routinely achieves MY objective while resulting in a both-win! Louis Pasteur put it this way, "Chance favors the prepared mind." So it is feasible and advisable to prepare for the interaction, perfecting what you will say and how you will respond. For professional salespeople this is typically called "pre-call planning".

I often tell professional salespeople that the days of winging it are over. It is not acceptable to just "show up and throw up." People are busy. They are wearing a lot of hats. We must honor them and utilize our limited time with them by preparing effectively. Preparing ahead of time is an ideal way to display to the other person how important they are, and how committed you are to discovering and meeting their wants and needs. And just think of the potential improvements this generates for your own time management. In my manufacturing experience, one of the first lessons in my career was, "If you don't have time to do it right the first time, when will you find time to do it over?"

Max Aiken, known as Lord Beaverbrook, informed us that Winston Churchill spent *days* planning his so-called impromptu speeches. Great quarterbacks like Peyton Manning practice their tactical offense plays repeatedly, before the game, to assure flawless execution on the field— during the game.

Preparing for your SELL Offense can be seen in this analogy from college basketball. During March Madness a few years ago one of the game analysts explained the coaching system of John Beilein, head coach of the Michigan Wolverines:

> *Beilein has turned a lot of programs around in very short order; 1-3 years to get a 20 win season. And he knows exactly what he wants to do both offensively and defensively. He calls his offense system "Organized Motion Offense," where the guys actually have to make reads---*
> *What are your teammates doing?*
> *What is the defense doing?*
> *And they make their cuts and screens based on that information. A lot of guys know how to "run plays" – but they don't know how to "play."*
> *John Beilein gets his guys to know how to play.*

In order to brilliantly execute your offense, it is essential to prepare before you go out on the court, the ice, the field, the sales call, the interaction.

My mission in unfolding the SELL Process to you in this book and my overriding purpose in every sales training camp I provide for sales professionals is to impart "game." I endeavor to effectively communicate this SELL

Process, both offense and defense, so that when you are in your *game* you are prepared, confident, and successful. The big plays will then present themselves and you will make them. Impressive stats will be your legacy.

Your SELL Process Planning Tool

I now introduce the SELL Process Planning Tool. From this point on, you will discover how to use this tool as a framework to prepare and execute highly effective selling. As you read this book it will help you imbed the learning as you apply the process at each step for an actual situation. I will instruct you at incremental points to put a bookmark in this book and tool out your process. Subsequently, the SELL process can be applied and utilized for each selling interaction you face.

The SELL Process Planning tool is available as a *free* download. This one-page Word template has text boxes for each step of the process. You may also print out the tool and complete it by hand. Take a moment now to download your SELL Process Planning Tool. Go to:

www.salesprofessionaltraining.com/selltools

When conducting sales training camps, an entire day of the course is spent on this tactical SELL Process. We examine each step of the SELL Process carefully. At each step, each salesperson writes out, in quotations, what they will say for that step of an actual customer call that they will be making shortly after the training. I run it like a "sales clinic" where we pick apart, correct, enhance, and wordsmith each person's attempt. Everyone shares and gets help from the workbinder, their peers, and the trainer. At the end of the day, each sales professional has a perfected pre-call plan for their "target" account. Usually we role-play that call. A scrimmage or dry run is unbelievably helpful in improving the tactical execution. The NFL watches a lot of film. They have a saying, "The eye in the sky doesn't lie!" When you see yourself on film it has a huge impact to help you personally up your game.

If you are a sales professional, the greatest impact is when this tool becomes a part of your daily regimen—pre-call planning appropriately for each sales call. Some calls may require a few minutes of preparation. Major, high-priority calls may demand significantly more. Eventually you can develop amazing on-your-feet selling skill. For the balance of your career, I expect that you will not even consider the option of skipping the discipline of pre planning your SELL Process. I personally will not pick up the phone, make a sales call, conduct an important meeting, or interact in an important dialog without tooling out my SELL sheet! If you sell for a living, masterful tactical selling is a must. As I mentioned earlier, that is where sales are won or lost, in that dynamic interaction between buyer and seller.

No matter what selling you engage in or how extensively you face selling situations, you can employ this book to help you make a real life application and really get the SELL Process embedded into your psyche! As I unfold each step of the SELL Process, you will be directed to make a real-world application using an upcoming interaction of your choice. This practical application as you learn the process, or *walk through your offense*, will facilitate the learning and assure that the process becomes more than book learning. The goal is that it becomes a natural part of your selling and daily interactions.

The importance of writing

First and foremost, please embrace the fact that writing is essential! I cannot emphasize enough the importance of writing as you prepare your SELL Process. I know some may be adverse to this due to a remnant agitation with scholastic challenges. (That is a clever way of saying you hated school.) Perhaps time pressures prevent you from considering another task to add to your plate. But give the discipline of writing a chance. It will be easier and become acceptable after you try it for a few situations and see how much better you do in the actual interaction. And don't panic! Your SELL Process writing is not for any eyes but yours. The exercise of writing is only to provide a cheat sheet for you. It can be typed, handwritten, or chicken-scratched (if you print like me).

How does writing help you?

- It is documented. When your process is written down, you can practice it and review it before the interaction. Delivery with ideal non-verbals and tone becomes achievable, consistently.

- Writing helps you remember. When you write, something happens in the brain, and it sticks. In one of my sales training events, a young sales professional shared a great analogy. He was a big bruiser, a former starting offensive lineman on his college football team. He confessed that he was no academic star. At one point he faced a test where a C grade or lower would make him ineligible for the next big game. His teacher gave him one grace for this difficult test. He was allowed to bring one page of notes. He proceeded to tell us that he studied hard, writing down every potential answer in tiny print until the entire page was virtually solid blue with ink. He proudly announced, "I aced it. Not a C, but an A." He added, "I'm no Einstein, but I hardly needed to use the notes. Then I realized that it was just like my football playbook. As one of the team captains, I wrote the plays, and they were now etched in my head. Plus, I *want* to remember my offense. I guess it's the same with tests . . . and tough selling interactions!"

· Writing allows creativity to flow. It provides time to consider new ideas, and catch and scrap the bad ones. Granted, we have all had a silver tongue when shooting from the hip in an interaction, but how often does that happen? Our best ideas are initiated, developed, and perfected over time, with careful thought.

· Writing helps you prioritize and stay focused on the right things.

· Writing helps you adapt your verbiage to the other person. It avoids the pitfall of talking from your perspective or personality style.

· Writing makes you EXACT. If you don't write it, you can't fix it.

Now let's eliminate a possible misconception that could dilute the credibility of writing out your SELL interaction plan.

The SELL Process Planning Tool is not a *script*, necessarily. Admittedly, in some applications such as repetitive phone selling, there may be some similarities to a script. But let's never condone mechanical, cold, scripted selling, but embrace a process that allows real human connection and interchange. The SELL Process Planning Tool is actually a conceptual outline of the expected dynamic interaction, with key elements defined and perfected! This is not "canned" selling. This is a process to enable well designed, well practiced, and well executed, professional selling—applied to each unique selling situation.

Planning is essential

Are you convinced that writing out your tactical plan before any selling interaction should be a discipline? I wholeheartedly hope so! I am passionate about this. I live it and teach it every day. And the more I teach it, the more I see it work, the more I'm convinced that this SELL Process is an essential tool for all. Take a moment to consider some reasons why this process—and using it as a framework to prepare—is so powerful.

1. Pre-planning with the SELL Process assures a better message. With careful thought ahead of time and

edited writing, your message will be clear and easy to absorb by the receiver. You are less likely to veer off on tangents or say stupid stuff that backfires. The message can also be tailored to them and their personality style.

2. Pre-planning with the SELL Process saves time. It helps you get to the point and keeps your objective clear. Plus, you minimize the chance that you will forget a critical point or question, having to return at a later time. Appropriate planning, focused on the other person, can actually make the interaction shorter. Have you ever engaged in a meeting that went in circles and never really landed? Interactions like those can leave the other person feeling like the interaction was all a waste of time.

3. Pre-planning with the SELL Process respects the other person. Pre-planning helps you focus on the other person and handle the interaction in a consultative way. People are busy. They are often short on time and under pressure. As for buyers, they are weary of motor-mouth salespeople wasting their time and bugging them to no end. And here is the good news. When you respect the other person and they recognize that it is about *them*, they will likely give you *more* time!

4. Pre-planning with the SELL Process presents a professional image. Unfortunately, selling has some lingering bad stigma. The proliferation of the SELL Process and a new focus on selling skills training can equip organizations to deliver a consultative,

solution-based approach to selling. When everyone who interacts with internal and external customers uses a professional process to skillfully interact, a good image can be enhanced for your company or brand.

5. Pre-planning with the SELL Process provides structure for good selling habits. If you are new at selling, preparing with the SELL Process will get you started on the right foot. For veterans (who can admittedly slip into ruts or bad habits), this logical process and the discipline of stopping to think and prepare corrects some costly slumps.

6. Pre-planning with the SELL Process is repeatable. This simple process can be used in any selling interaction across the board. That reality is what drove the writing of this book! You can use it in any interaction, at any stage in a simple or complex selling cycle, in any industry or day-to-day situation. It is also repeatable in the sense that once you develop a SELL Process plan for a particular type of interaction, it can be repeated. Similar calls or situations can become models or templates. For example, lists of similar, repetitive sales phone calls can utilize a standardized SELL sheet. The process can be adapted to variations but employ the proven phraseology that has been tweaked and polished. This application takes telesales to a whole new level of effectiveness!

7. Pre-planning with the SELL Process allows team selling and coaching. Sadly, most sales teams seem

to evolve into an independent, lone-dog mentality. Sales veterans set the standard and perform in a vacuum. New sales rookies are often "thrown to the wolves" to figure it out as they go. The school of hard knocks costs more and takes excessively more time than training with this hands-on tool! When this tool is standardized, everyone is on the same page. Just think of the implications in the supply channel. Joint sales calls and interactions as a team, are workable. Cross-pollination and team synergy is cultivated. Leaders and mentors have a process or system to use as a framework for individual critique and improvement. Coaching is implemented in place of cheerleading or punishing. The possibilities are limited only by how far you choose to integrate this tool.

8. Pre-planning with the SELL Process works! It gets the result, the desired action—the sale. I have taught this for decades and the proof is there. Try it, and you will be a believer.

In a major address at the 1940 NALU (National Association of Life Underwriters) annual convention in Philadelphia, the late Albert Gray made this powerful statement:

"The common denominator of success . . . lies in forming the habit of doing things that failures don't like to do."

Decide on your target selling situation and let's get to work learning and applying the SELL Process.

Know your objective

Before you embark on filling out your first SELL sheet, before you ever pick up your pencil, and by all means before you darken the door of any sales interaction, you must establish your objective. Why is it so important to have a purpose for the call or interaction? Well, as we established earlier in this book, the activity of selling is a proactive interaction that has a goal. It is not merely discussion. If you don't know where you are going, how will you know when you get there? Having an objective in selling is paramount. Your objective keeps you focused and actually guides your preparation and delivery throughout the process. Your Start, the questions you ask, what you cover, and the action you ask for, are all derived from a clear, action-oriented objective.

Understand that your objective depends totally on the situation. Some salespeople boast that their objective is always to get an order and close the sale. This is not realistic in many complex, long, selling cycles in which numerous decision-makers are involved. The objective for a particular SELL interaction is simply the next logical incremental action that is desired for this encounter. It should be appropriately assertive, yet realistic and rational. Set high goals by all means, because this powerful process equips you to accomplish more than you might have previously expected. But be flexible and reasonable, maintaining your objective while you keenly assess the dialog to adjust if needed. Pro quarterbacks have great plays in their game plan, but the savvy to read the defense and call a correct audible at the line of scrimmage separates the good from the great. I have seen individuals learn the SELL Process and in their first role-play or customer interaction they begin to show OCD tendencies as they barrel through their SELL plan of action. It is normal to be a bit choppy when we learn a good offense. The balance comes with extensive practice and experience in the SELL Process.

The primary factor in establishing your objective for the interaction or call is that it must be *action-oriented*. If no action or change results, then you really didn't sell. Be wary of the normal inclination to be vague or 'wishy-washy' about this primary determination, just seeing how it goes or hoping to get something done.

Ricky Page titled one of his books *Hope is Not a Strategy*. I love that phrase. And I think Colin Powell stated it succinctly when he said, "Define your victory." My emphasis on this is in response to years of training salespeople in which I have observed that this crucial starting point in selling seems universally weak! I have heard vague objectives like, "My objective is to heal the relationship." My response to that is, "OK, sounds noble, but what does that look like? What will the customer do as a result of this call that will demonstrate that you got that done? What is the action?" Avoid ineffectual objectives like, "to prove my solution is better," "to grow and expand my business," "to present my product," "to do more with this customer," or "to get them to agree with me."

I know that the diversity of selling situations is expansive, but to give you a general understanding, here are a few better examples:

- to get the next meeting set with a specific person at a documented time.

- · to agree on a trial and Lock a second meeting to move forward when the trial succeeds.

- · to place an order.

- · to get specs for a proposal or quote.

- · to take some incremental action that leads to the ultimate goal of both parties.

Keep in mind that with an action-oriented objective in place, the steps of the SELL Process allow you to not only get the primary objective accomplished, but discover new information, set the stage for the next meeting, learn about what is important to the other person, build relationship and trust, and prove your proposed benefits and value.

Until you are proficient in honing in on the action-oriented objective for your selling interactions, perhaps you can use the following easy litmus test. After deciding on your sales call or interaction objective, test it with the question: "as evidenced by . . .?"

Decide on the action that you want, and it will guide your SELL pre-planning and keep your interaction focused and productive. What do you want the other person to DO?

Apply the process

 Write out your objective on the line specified at the top of your SELL Process Planning sheet.

Chapter 3
Start—to attract

This first step of the SELL Process is when you initiate the interaction and take control. It is your inbounds play. The Start is where you attract the other person to your objective. Of course, there are situations or sales assignments in which selling interactions are *reactive*, such as retail or counter sales. Or when another person strikes up a conversation in which you have a secondary agenda to ask for some action or request a change. Either way, at some point if you are to sell, you need to skillfully take the helm and set the direction of the interaction toward your objective. You attract the other person to this with a very carefully prepared Start.

The Start is typically no more than a few sentences or a concise introduction with a statement or question. It lasts, perhaps, a fraction of a minute and ideally you transition seamlessly into the next step: Evaluate. But those brief moments are huge. If you can't get the ball in play, you will never score. And most importantly, this first impression is of utmost concern. This step sets the tone for the rest of the interaction. The customer or other person may be thinking, "Who let this one in?" "So what are you trying to push?" or "Oh no, another salesperson." In many situations they may welcome your conversation and be eager for or open to what you have to offer. But either way, this is the play of the game, and you had better be ready. Don't blow this opportunity. If you are not prepared, or say the wrong thing in the wrong way to Start, it may be an uphill battle to recover control and credibility. The unique part about this step is that it is *all yours*. You can say anything you want in any way you want. The other steps of the process from here on out are somewhat dependent upon the responses and reactions of the other person, but the Start is up to you. So do the prudent thing and write it out; perfect it.

I have conducted workshops on this step with thousands of salespeople, both rookie and veteran, and invariably the exercise of writing out their first attempt at a Start is a shocking revelation. They often find that it is difficult and challenging. They sometimes try so hard that they make it harder than it needs to be. But you will discover that this is part of the learning process as you begin to do the discipline of writing out what you want to say. The intent is not to make it wordy or clever, but to make it effective and appropriate. This will come with practice and creativity.

As you grapple with some of your first attempts to write out a good Start, consider this: if it is this hard—when I can take my time and develop the right wording—how could I expect to do this on the fly in front of the customer?

Understanding the Start

So what should the Start look like? I submit that, as a rule, it should be short, sweet, and to the point. Simple is best. It should be based on the objective and should direct toward the desired action. However, that does not imply that the Start should be blatantly aggressive or obvious. You need to decide what approach is proper based on the situation, your personality, and the other person involved. You see, there is no silver bullet or pat answer as to what your Start should be. As I began this book, I informed you that I had no plans to tell you what to say or to spoon feed canned statements or responses. Only *you* can figure it out, but I will help you and give you the framework. Galileo Galilei said, "We cannot teach people anything; we can only help them discover it within themselves." I love it when I get people thinking—creating better things to say! Can you see why I hate classic, overworked sales approaches and hokey pick up lines?

Overworked Sales Approaches:
"You shouldn't buy from them, you should buy from me."
"I just happened to be in the area and thought I'd stop by."
"I'm your new rep. Here's what we do...Blah, Blah, Blah, Blah, Blah . . . thanks. Call me."

Hokey Pick-up lines:
"I lost my number, can I have yours?"
"Are you from Tennessee? 'Cause you're the only ten I see".
"If I asked you to go out with me, would it be the same answer as this question?" (*Actually this one is genius. Either 'yes' or 'no' responses work. Clever, but sort of smart aleck.*)

And by all means, quit using this one for either:
"I've got a couple things I'd like to show you."

Let's think of some new things to say! Question everything you have been doing.

Now, as a sidebar, let's discuss the inclusion of small talk. This is another element of the upcoming interaction that you really should consider ahead of time. Some people like and need to be warmed up with personal or light conversation like weather, family, or sports. Others want to get right to business and may see small talk as a waste of time or a blemish on your credibility. Try to anticipate this and make a good decision. Avoid controversial topics. Then, as you begin, stay alert and attentive to non-verbals, tone, and little comments. Be poised to abort the small talk if it doesn't hit the mark, then move right into the *big* talk. The big talk is your prepared Start!

There is nothing worse than an oblivious salesperson or some other individual who approaches another with obnoxious, excessive small talk, going on and on, blind to the subtle rejection and thinking erroneously they are a "relationship builder." (I call this diarrhea of the mouth.) What a way to sabotage credibility and distract from the selling task at hand! Use wisdom in deciding how much or how little is right for the person and situation.

The Start is where you attract to the objective and set the direction. You get the other person's attention and jump-start the process. Having that arrow in your quiver before you begin equips you for an interaction that will hit the mark. Once the small talk tapers or ends and when eyes are on you saying in essence, "Why are you here?" you are ready. Ready to SELL!

What, in addition to small talk, should be considered or investigated before your Start? Wow. When you take a moment to think about it, there is so much that should be considered before deciding on that all-important Start. Most professional salespeople are embarrassed when they think of how many times they just walked in and shot from the hip. Below are just a few of the things to take into account. You can add more based on your selling situations and particulars. Bottom-line: you have much to consider in order to design and execute an ideal Start that really "nails it!"

You should consider:

- Your objective.

- The other person's values, opinions, and tendencies.

- The personality and behavior style of this person.

- Past history with this person or company.

- Where you are in the selling cycle and how feasible a final decision is now.

- What happened in your previous interactions or calls.

- Organizational politics and others involved.

- Power and decision-making authority.

- Current capacity, availability, and performance of you, your product, or service.

- Time and location of this meeting and possible distractions.

So let's do this. Next, before I cut you loose to write out this first step on your SELL Process Planning Tool, I will provide some basic varieties or examples of Starts. Then, you can insert a bookmark and take your first shot at writing your Start for your selected target situation or sales call.

Types of Starts

There are many ways to start a sales call. Every situation and contact is unique. The basic classifications I will provide you now are designed to give you a basis and get your creative juices flowing. These are initial tools for your toolbox. Keep adding to these and perfecting different ones that work for you. Choose the right tool for the right job. Eventually, you will become a proficient "journeyman" in sales. This step is all yours and you must make it count! Your pre-planning is essential. You are the sales doctor. It is your responsibility to design a Start that will be ideal for the particular interaction at hand.

As you read the classifications to follow, think about scenarios and selling situations that you face. Think of some specific examples for each classification that relate to your world. Mull over when and when *not* to use each one. Keep in mind that you really know each pending situation and all the complexity around them better than anyone. You are best suited to decide on an appropriate Start.

Confident Start—In some situations this type of Start is excellent. Perhaps you are confident that a solution can be worked out together. Maybe you have experience, expertise, or proven successes that you want to articulate as you start. In some cases, starting with a confident statement or phrase can provide relief for the receiver or even impress them. Be careful though. As with any of the following types of Starts, there are always cases where it may not work or may even be disastrous. Confident Starts could sound cocky or presumptuous. Some might border on sounding like you are delusional to the situation at hand. Think it out. You are the sales doctor.

Compliment Start—This one is a favorite of some folks. I had a guy tell me he *always* starts with a compliment. He said, "People love to be stroked and praised. It opens them up to you." He does have a valid point. My warning though is clear. Don't "*always*" or "*never*" do anything! In this classification of Starts, beginning with a compliment may actually come off as schmoozing or sucking-up. It might hint to a bit of fear on your part as you appear to say nice things before you go to the ugly stuff.

Gift Start—This type of start has equally as much concern. Many professional salespeople have suggested elimination of this Start due to the stigma related to old-school salesmen who dropped off advertising specialties and candy in an effort to approach customers. But don't throw this out just yet. There are cases when beginning with a gift can be the ticket. Many tough situations—cold calls, lobby visits, or walk-ins—have had the contact disarmed by a simple, thoughtful gift. As a rule, based on comments of a host of sales professionals through the years, most would say a gift is usually best offered at the *end* of a conversation or meeting instead of using it to start. It leaves a gentle, good reminder and rewards productive interaction. But again, you make the choice.

Puppy Dog Start—Boy, I like this one and why not use it if it applies? If the interaction has you in an obvious situation where one would naturally feel sorry for you, it may be to your advantage to start with something about that. Avoid groveling, and don't carry it too far; but if it fits for you, OK. Even humor or a hint of sarcasm has been known to break down initial walls. Again, the key to all of these Starts is to contemplate the pending interaction, scope the situation—then decide and write.

Referral Start—Dropping the name of a person that the other person respects or knows is quite often effective. In certain situations, especially in professional sales calling, this tool may be required for some potential clients. There are some people who will not even talk with a vendor unless you are referred. This may be due to the fact that some buyers are inundated with solicitors, but the reality remains that starting with a reference is at times the only way to attract. However, I think the caution here is evident. Referrals can be your worst nightmare in some cases, so do your background research and be aware of the pitfalls associated with this classification of Starts.

Benefit Start—People change their thinking and take action based on perceiving benefits for themselves. Discovering and persuasively presenting benefits to the other person is a core fundamental of selling and the SELL Process. You will see this in step three of the SELL Process: Leverage. For now, understand that there are times when presenting a known or highly probable benefit to the other person in the Start can be the primo way to attract them. As quickly as I offer that, I need to remind you that *less* is better in the Start. Starting with a benefit may open your floodgates and tempt you to slip right into your presentation, answer, or solution, and the Start is way too early for that! One more note, if it may be an advantage to use a key benefit *at the end* of the interaction to incentivize the Lock, why burn it up now? If you have heeded these warnings and you still feel that starting with a benefit is the right thing, by all means do it.

Firm Statement Start—This type works extremely well in the right situation, with the right type of person. Task-oriented people or "type A" personalities may respond well when someone gets right to the point and makes a firm statement. Just say it and let them react. If you are lucky, the other person will admire your grit and give you a rare chance that he or she may not normally give to most. Control emotion and practice to minimize non-verbals that may be offensive or condescending. Steer clear of what I call *fighting words*. These Starts result in a possible hanging lull after delivery so be prepared with a follow-up or a salvage attempt. As you might expect, the risk with this type of Start is high and should be carefully calculated. Use sparingly. Try it when you have nothing left to lose. Be sure to have a "plan B" if it derails, and trust me—do not burn your bridges.

Shocking Statement Start—This is a firm statement on steroids. Believe it or not, I have used a few of these and they have worked. Sometimes people just need a zap to shock them out of their neutrality. Again, very seldom, but when you have weighed the risk and considered the situation, a shocking statement may be just the prescription.

Question Start—This may be one of your better ways to begin. Starting with a question gets the other person talking right out of the gate, and that is a beautiful thing. It sets you up as a consultant and puts the focus on the other person allowing them to share what is important to them, paving the way to move right into the next essential step: Evaluate. That's all good! Before you default to using this type of Start, be aware that in some cases the other person may not trust you enough yet to begin disclosing information. A question is powerful, but in the Start, it may intimidate or make the recipient feel like they are on the witness stand or in a deposition. We will get some good learning and practice on the skill of asking questions in the next chapter. After you get that under your belt, you will be much better equipped to design and confirm the usage of a question for the Start step. One future advantage that you will find when you have some experience in pre-planning, is that when you are writing out your open-ended and closed-ended questions for step two of the SELL Process, sometimes you craft a standout question that presents itself as the ultimate question to ask in the Start. So you move it up on your sheet. That's when you say, "I am so glad I invested the time to prepare before this interaction. I'm gonna nail this meeting!"

Agenda Start—I have used the tar out of this one. In your opening statement, especially if your interaction happens to be to a group, you Start with a concise rundown of how the meeting will go. For example: "This is an important meeting, and I am prepared to make it worth your time. First I need to ask you some questions and truly understand your needs and the specs. With that understanding I can show you some valuable options and our proposed solution(s). Then we can decide the next step and move forward together." Do you notice how subtly that Start unveils the SELL Process? It stifles the fear that you will "present your brains out" and heads that remorse off at the pass. It also gently assumes permission to ask probing questions and get the required information. Best of all, it lets them know that we are not leaving without action and forward progress. If you are there to do business and quarterback the meeting, this is an authoritative Start! Oh, and feel free to add a transition statement, question, benefit or any other Start component on the end. The variations on this theme are limited only by your creativity and tenacity. (Just be sure not to slide down the 'presentation' chute and do a selling monologue!)

Product or Service Start—For salespeople of any industry, this one can come into play. Attractive offers, exceptional service, or proprietary products can sometimes be the right way to start an interaction. The caveat here is to be extremely careful not to do this habitually or slip into the stereotypical salesperson. Everyone says their product or service is better.

Similar Example Start—If you have solved a problem for someone else, if you have seen precisely what you are addressing in this interaction before—and have successfully dealt with it—this may be your choice of Starts. Included would be industry expertise, past victories with that person, a similar customer or situation. You may even describe an expected need and how you consistently resolve it. The goal here is to get undivided attention by attracting them to something that is important to them at the time. If this Start fits, use it. Draft out what you will say and perfect it.

Be creative! You can mix and match any of these as well as any others you come up with. All that matters is that you use the right Start based on the situation and the other person you are dealing with.

Apply the process

 Using the examples just given, and your own creativity, develop the Start for your target situation and write it in the Start space on your SELL Process sheet. *Write it in quotations.*

Improvement and refinement of your Starts

OK, now that you are finished with your first draft of your Start, read it back and put yourself in the customer's shoes.

Earlier in this chapter, I indicated that this first step of the SELL Process is huge! Therefore, I will attempt to help you critique and revise as necessary to make sure it is your best shot. As a rule, your first shot is not your best shot. A critical eye as you get comfortable writing out your SELL Offense will allow your selling skill to go to a new level. You will find that the subsequent steps are much easier once you painstakingly break through the daunting barrier of the Start step. I have worked intently through this with thousands of sales professionals in training camps, and I assure you that once you craft the right Start, deliver it in the interaction, and see it's power, the experience will be an epiphany for you.

Read your Start back again. If you can, read it to a colleague or trusted peer.

Is it the right length?

Remember: as a rule, less is usually better. Short and to the point is a good guideline. The more you say, the more risk there is that you will start into your solution or veer off onto a tangent. One of the most common errors I see in sales interactions of any kind is that the person selling starts off with too much too fast. This overwhelms the other person and gives them way more information than they can even process or absorb. The response is usually a stunned or annoyed stare, which triggers even more rhetoric. Keep it simple and short. Write it out, perfect it, practice it, and stick to it! There are times when a longer Start is necessary, and in those cases you will know, if you have taken the time to think it through and pre-plan your tactics. A long letter written by Ben Franklin to a colleague said this at the end: "I'm sorry about the long letter . . . I did not have time to make it shorter."

Is it real?

Here is another important editing criteria. Be yourself. Be sincere. Make sure your Starts don't sound like the canned, overworked lingo of a typical salesperson. Feel free to use your own wording and style. Don Buttrey did not write this book to tell you what to say. I want to help you make this process your own. Some of the best Starts I hear are gut-level and address the situation precisely without being wordy or pompous. When someone brings a Start to me for input and it sounds all flowery, I usually ask,

"OK, now what is the situation again?" They proceed to fill me in on who it is and what happened up to this point. They will then give me a simple statement about what they *really* want to say to the person. Often, that is exactly what they should have written for their Start and I say, "That's it. Use that. You asked for help because deep in your mind you knew what you had written was fake." And they grab their pencil and rewrite it before they lose it again! I am convinced that if you work on your SELL Process and bust down your paradigms, you have what it takes to be really good at selling. That is why I love my job.

Is the focus on the other person?

Now this is a tough edit. If you write out a Start that is really about *you* and what you want, and then read it back to yourself over and over, it can wax precious. You can easily miss the subtle self-centeredness. If you wrote words that make *you* feel better or that cater to your way of doing business, it may only work if you were selling to yourself! We naturally have a tendency to word things from our own perspective, for example:

"I would really like you to . . . "

"We really want to do more with you . . . "

"Our organization offers great . . . "

These sound harmless and maybe no one would notice if you used them. True. That is exactly why writing your Start out ahead of time with a sincere effort to focus your process on the other person will set you apart and amazingly improve effectiveness and results! Try wording like:

"Taking action will assure that you . . . "

"From what your partner experienced, expanding
to do more will provide you with . . . "
"Based on the service you must have it makes sense
to . . . "

Please, only take the above examples at face value to help you latch on to the concept. The application is as extensive as the people reading this book.

Does it fit the particular person?

Not only should the focus be on the other person, but the type or classification of the Start you choose also needs to fit the other person's style. For example, if they are a task-oriented type of person who is decisive and to the point, it may make better sense to use a firm statement or confident Start. Of course, this is by no means a hard, fast rule. Nevertheless, if they actually admire assertiveness and utilize conflict, but you abhor it, you will need to stretch yourself and make some radical adaptations to your Start if you want to connect with a person who is way different than you.

Let me offer a suggestion for further study and personal improvement. There are four orientations of human beings, based on significant study of human psychology and the powerful concept of DISC Theory. In my Relationship Model, (which is part of my sales training curriculum) I term the four orientations of people as Task-, Creative-, Fact-, and People-oriented. Adjusting your personal style and adapting your methods of interaction to the style of the person you are selling to, is an extremely valuable ability. Do some study on the theory of the four quadrants of people related to DISC Theory. It may really help you in your selling.

Is it positive?

When you read back your first draft, keep a keen eye out for negativity. Avoid Starts that back-peddle or that smell of low self-esteem. You are selling, and you don't want to defeat yourself from the get-go. Don't apologize for the meeting, as that tends to minimize the importance of your value in persuading a change or action. This leads to negative confessions like, "I know you are busy," and "you may not agree," or other such defeating Starts. Believe it or not, I have ceased to "thank" the other person for meeting with me. (Whoops. Half of you probably looked at your initially written Start and said, "Oh snap.") Hey, I'm all about courtesy, but in the Start—my shot in getting this thing moving where I want—that overused approach simply says, "You are doing this as a favor for me and I am an interruption that you tried to avoid until I bugged you enough to get in front you." I exaggerated in this example to show my point. If you can't think of a positive statement then perhaps your situation calls for starting with a carefully worded question. You may be surprised that the response reveals that they are not seeing the situation as negatively as you feared! Give your objective a fair chance, and Start on a positive note.

Is it based on your objective?

Truly, the Lock step and reaching your objective and a both-win result begins with the Start step. As the process indicates, you Start—to *attract*. You attract to the goal or clear, action-oriented objective of the call or meeting. Does your Start get this conversation moving down the path that you want, or at least facing the right direction? If it does that suitably, it could range anywhere between glaring and faint. Again, you must decide. The stakes could be high.

Now, back to the drawing board. Revise and wordsmith your drafted Start to a realistic point where you feel it will have the highest likelihood of success with the other person. Don't get frustrated. Don't make it too hard. The best Starts are often basic and simple. If you slip over to clever or cute Starts it may lead to trouble anyway. You will get notably better from now on if you have the personal discipline to pre-plan as a regimen. Keep reminding yourself of how improvement in this SELL Process will impact your relationships, and if you are a career salesperson, your income.

One more thing, practice your tone and non-verbal kinesics. According to research by Al Mehrabian at UCLA, words are 7 percent of a message and you have already begun to see the dramatic impact that wording has. Tone is 38 percent of the message, and non-verbal kinesics a whopping 55 percent of communication. Closely integrated with effective SELL Process interaction is the mastery of communication skills. Thus, another facet of your personal improvement plan is to study and incorporate communication awareness and skill into your SELL Process!

Let's move on to step two of the SELL Process: Evaluate. The Start step is huge, but this next step is universally attributed as the most crucial element in selling.

Chapter 4

Evaluate—to discover interests

Asking questions is the finest skill in selling. It is the discipline of seasoned veterans. You absolutely cannot sell at the highest level of effectiveness if you do not utilize probing questions as you Evaluate the customer and the situation. Logically, you cannot engage in step three, Leverage, if you have not interacted in this step adequately. Do not skip this step. How in the world can you know how they might benefit or what desire will trigger conviction to action if you don't find out by skillfully asking questions? The obvious reasons for Evaluation are to discover facts, understand needs, confirm assumptions, learn about motivations, and reveal objections. Some of the less visible reasons are equally important—getting the other person engaged, letting them talk about themselves (people love to do that), and exposing unknown variables that you would not even think to ask about. The beauty of skillful dialog using well-crafted questions is that it allows the other person to speak the things that otherwise you might have leveraged yourself. When *they* speak it, *they own* it! Even if you already researched ahead of time, know the person very well, or previously asked questions of this person, it still behooves you to prepare and ask questions. Things might have changed. The person may have second thoughts. Who knows? In your last meeting they may have felt threatened or intimidated and under this duress provided less than honest or complete information.

I may seem a bit adamant about the critical nature of this step, yet nearly every sales training book or course emphasizes it and the people I have trained agree quickly to its importance. What has become evident is that we seem to know the importance of asking questions, but in practice we fail to do it adequately. I used the pronoun "we" because, yes, I too am guilty as charged. We are so often tempted to skip this step or quickly abort it due to a host of reasons (not excuses). Here are a few:

- We assume. (And some of you know what that can spell.) Assumptions blind us from hints of new information that may pop up in the dialog.

- We think we know the answer. And maybe we *do* have the answer, so we nervously gush it out because we can't hold it until we are ready for step three.

- We get too enthusiastic or excited about the next step.

· We get nervous or uncomfortable with the mild tension caused by pauses or non-verbals after we serve a question.

· We fail to prepare primary questions and by default go down our path of least resistance, rambling on incessantly.

· We have not developed or tapped into the disciplines of patience and listening.

The path to mastering this step is self-control and the discipline of laying out the appropriate questions and letting them do the work. If you master the Evaluate step, selling gets easier and easier. No longer will you depend simply on your persuasiveness alone. The truth, (what they speak and divulge), will set you free. No more guessing. No more *selling in the dark*.

Ask more questions . . . !

One time I was asked what I do for a living. I replied, "I guess I teach salespeople to shut up." I have seen thousands of video-recorded role-plays. Trust me, excessive talking and not asking enough questions *is* a problem. I even considered a Buttrey bobblehead that implies "shut-up" with every nod. That is why I teach this responsive mantra to salespeople. I say, "Ask more questions . . . " and they reply, "and shut up." I try to drive this home in any training I provide. I want you to say that over and over in your head.

Ask more questions . . . and shut up!

Ask more questions . . . and shut up!
Ask more questions . . . and shut up!
Ask more questions . . . and shut up!

Perhaps if you brainwash yourself by repetition you can create a new trigger in your brain to . . . *ask more questions . . . and shut up!* Burn it into your brain. It will serve you well.

When I played basketball in high school I would get all excited when I happened to get a rebound in a momentous point of the game. I would dribble like a madman to the other end of the court and throw up some wild shot against four defenders. My coach would yell on the sidelines this one phrase that he tried to drive into my head:

"Slow down and set up your offense!"

In selling, your offense is the next step. Slow down. Relax. Control the pace with poised dialog including well-crafted questions and intuitive follow-up probing. This is how you set up your offense in selling (which we will unfold in the next chapter about Leverage).

Here is our challenge in this chapter: I want to help you learn how to ask good questions. I wish it were as simple as giving you a technique and teaching you a methodology for asking questions. A technique of any type is risky and could never encompass every theoretical interaction represented by the readers of this book. The worst part is that a technique would undoubtedly make the other person feel manipulated—like they were on the witness stand or in a deposition. They might suspect that they are being taken advantage of. At some later point this can develop into what is known as, "buyer's remorse."

I have discovered that the ability to ask questions in this step of the process is simultaneously as basic and profound as these four principles:

1. Prepare well-crafted questions and use them in the interaction.

2. Make a conscious mental effort to listen.

3. Bolster a desire to understand the other person.

4. Cultivate an inquisitive mind.

Once we carefully look at these four principles, you will be ready to begin a journey of becoming a skillful evaluator. Understand this out of the gate: it is a developed skill.

Prepare well-crafted questions and use them in the interaction.

There are two fundamental types of questions:

First, open-ended questions are questions which can't be answered with a simple yes or no response. These types of questions force the other person to think. They have an almost undeniable ability to engage another person and get them talking. Open-ended questions are ideal for revealing facts, opinions, needs, wants, feelings, emotions, and priorities, just to name a few. Use these liberally to assure wide-open dialog. Many times the wider they are, the better they are at getting information and unfiltered particulars. Examples might begin with: *why, what, how, tell me* (one of my favorites), *explain*, etc. When utilizing these powerful questions, avoid designing them as multiple-choice. I have found that it is better to ask a more general, wide open question and let them go down the path or paths that they choose, without skewing or presupposing their thoughts. If they give you a deer-in-the-headlight stare you can always prod afterward with a few suggestions to prime the pump.

Secondly, closed-ended questions solicit a yes, no, or maybe response. Often they are returned with short answers or small pieces of requested information. They have an important place in the Evaluate step as they can qualify the direction or path. Closed-ended questions can confirm or even eliminate items or possible options under consideration. They work effectively as follow-ups to open-ended questions that exposed a series of issues. Often, closed-ended questions are technical and logical in nature. I have noticed that technical or engineering-minded people are proficient at using these—sometimes to their own detriment—by circumventing or overlooking the value of open-ended questions. Examples might begin with: *who, when, should, how much, do, did*, etc. These are effective questions, but proper use in tandem with more open questions is the art you want to refine. Best of all, these are your ideal choice when it is time to finalize, close, or Lock in the action. Ask directly and get commitment. Just be careful not to use these when an open-ended question is the ideal choice. For example, I would not suggest the question, "Are you the decision maker?" This implies that if the person is not, you are wasting your time. It also caters to the folks who are decision-maker wannabes. They will snap out a bogus "yes" in a heartbeat if they need self-validation saying, "Yes, and at home too!" Some may be too embarrassed to say no. Or they might simply say yes, leaving you back in the spotlight to scramble for a better follow-up question. This is just one example in which a closed-ended question is not the tool of choice. Perhaps something like, "Tell me about the decision-making process in your organization" might result in the real scoop. Indirect questions like that discreetly bring out more and better information. They are less offensive or threatening and tend to preserve the trust needed for continued disclosure. Of course, effectiveness varies based on the behavior style of the other person. Admittedly a few isolated people respond well to blunt, direct questions. Go figure. Yes, again, *you* have to figure out what has the highest chance for success in each selling interaction you conduct!

With some effort and a persistent desire to get better at asking questions you can! I have been pleased to find that most educated people are pretty good at coming up with effective questions. In fact, very shortly you will write out your questions on step two of your SELL Process Planning Tool. You will see as we continue, that the real challenge is to deliver and utilize the questions you create properly in the interaction.

Let me first model a simple progression that may be helpful in setting the stage for your own creative improvement of typical questions. Variations of a few typical questions may inspire you to think outside the box and create some powerful questions of your own. Keep in mind that although I am employing a classic "sales" example, the logic applies for whatever you might face. Revise the words to incorporate situations or selling that you engage in.

"What do you like about your current supplier?"

Do you see the potential risk here? The response may leave you with an uphill battle. This is open-ended for sure, but it begs for a list of good qualities about what is actually your competitor. Now who is selling to whom? This is probably not the best strategy. Ok then let's try this . . .

"What problems are you having?"

Again, open-ended, but do you see the danger? This implies that the other person is in fact having problems or even doing things wrong. It reeks of mud slinging. It is sort of negative. Even without any negative baggage, it puts all the pressure on the other person to figure it out and tell you how to fix it. Isn't that why you are there? Maybe we can do better . . .

"What are some pluses and minuses about your current vendor (or situation)?"

Much better. This allows them to address good or bad things (or both), depending on what is on the tip of their brain. I like the revision. One fly in the ointment, however, is that this is still talking about the competition. This type of question can perhaps provide good information, but it would be prudent not dwell on competitors or use up our discussion time in that vein! Your call—but let me offer another variation on this theme . . .

"Tell me what you look for in a supplier/partner."

Whoa baby, now we are crafting a great question. And how about this follow-up . . .

"What are your selection criteria?"

This stimulates the other person to disclose their desires, opinions, and views. They might even offer info about what they are NOT getting—that they *want!* That slip of shared knowledge may have never been let go had you asked the more pointed questions earlier in our example. This can be taken to yet another level if it applies . . .

"Once we start serving you, what will you expect from my company? From me as your contact?"

Now who is the focal point of discussion? You! This is subtle without even a hint of manipulation. You are in control. That is what the SELL Process is all about.

I love the art of crafting great questions. Still, keep in mind that some of the best questions are intrinsically simple. Great dialog and a ton of information can result from questions as basic as:

"Fill me in on the decision making process."
"Help me understand what led to this."
"Describe how that impacted you." or
"What are your thoughts on _____?"

Apply the process

 Now take some quality time to write out 4-8 open-ended questions in the Evaluate space on your SELL Process sheet. Make sure they are well-crafted and finalize them in quotations with precise wording. You may also choose to list some closed-ended questions or bullets of key information that you must uncover in the interaction.

After you finish writing, read the questions back and revise them if they need to be opened up or tweaked a bit. I expect that when you read them back or share them with an associate you will be gratified with your work. Each one will hold a wealth of potential for facilitating a rewarding interaction. In fact, over time you will see that some of the questions you create can be used over and over again. Some may merely need minor adaptation. Others can be used straight up the same way each time. I know I have my own pet questions that serve me well. You can share your effective questions with other team members if you are part of a sales team and borrow good ones that you pick up from veterans. Plagiarism in sales is a wonderful thing. This kind of mutual help and cross-pollination is a rare but rewarding thing among sales teams.

In fact, in a sales-team environment or even for your own personal benefit, you can document great questions and build part of your SELL Offense Playbook. I have even seen some teams build primary qualifying questions into their customer profile page, or integrate them right into their CRM database for consistent use by all. Proven technical or product-related questions can be included for a wide range of market segments or customer types. When you begin to recognize all of these potential implementations, it is easy to understand why so many companies have standardized the use of the SELL Process in their sales organizations!

Now that you have your questions written and ready for the actual dynamic interaction, we need to reinforce the next three principles. Great selling is not as simple as just asking a good list of questions, getting some surface answers, and then jumping right to the next step—presenting your answer, solution, or *case*, so to speak. This step will take some skill in execution. That reminds me of what coach John McKay replied when asked what he thought about his team's execution. "I'm in favor of it," he said. We all, including even experienced sales people, need to get better at the Evaluate step. Here is the next vital principle.

Make a conscious mental effort to listen.

The SELL Process embodies communication. Therefore, to succeed in this process, we must master the skills of communication, of which listening is the better half, and more. I often remind myself that I was designed with *two* ears and *one* mouth. The ears cannot close, the mouth can. Enough said!

Improvement in communication begins with accepting that there is no magic formula or proverbial list of 10 self-help tips that will turn you into a better communicator. Communication is a dynamic interaction between infinitely unique human beings. Thus, it requires a *heightened awareness* in order to make it better. When you are keenly aware of the things that will hinder or destroy communication, you logically become a better communicator. Many of the concepts that will help you develop communication skills are basics that have been known and taught for years. It makes sense, as we work on the Evaluate step of the SELL Process, that we overview these basics.

Awareness of *filters* is a good starting point. When you say something to someone else or they speak to you, the message is filtered through your brain as you attempt to decode it or figure out the meaning and intent. Filters can evolve from things like prejudices, religion, upbringing, background, education, and really any factor in a person's life that might be used to process the incoming data. It encompasses a person's understanding and worldview. The issue is that all of us are different—some are diametrically different than others. I am sure that you can think of a host of situations in which you said something and someone heard a completely different thing than you intended. So, we hear things from our own perspective or point of view. We are doing it. The other person is doing it. How do we overcome this hurdle in communication? Well the answer is simple but the doing is hard. It simply takes *more* feedback and *more* dialog. Work at facilitating the back-and-forth interaction. Ask. Confirm. Questions like, "So what I hear you saying is_____?" can help clear up filter-caused confusion. Always remember: you have no idea what is really going on in the other person's brain and heart. The only way to find out is to . . . wait for it . . . "Ask more questions" . . . (and shut up!).

Awareness of *kinesics* is another step toward better communication. Kinesics is defined as: *1) the study of certain body movements which interact with thoughts and feelings to complete the communication cycle. 2) human non-verbal communication. 3) vibes.*

Kinesics are such an important aspect of communication. For example, consider the scope of possible word connotations. In the English language the same word or phrase can often mean completely different things! At times, the same exact word carries *opposite* meanings. Perhaps the intended meaning is implied by the situation, but the actual interpretation is always decoded in the mind of the receiving party. Voice tone is another aspect of kinesics that can change the intended message substantially. Body language carries the most significance. Body language includes postures, gestures, facial clues, and even personal space, intertwined with what is spoken. These elements of communication can result in a complex concoction to decipher! As alluded to earlier in this book, kinesics and body language comprise the bulk of communication. It is always good to keep the perspective that words are 7 percent of the communication and that tone and non-verbals are a total of 93 percent (38 and 55 percent respectively)! Kinesics have some typical meanings but you really never know the precise meaning at hand until you connect with and begin to really understand the other person that you are dealing with. Further study of body language and kinesics is highly recommended. For the purpose of applying this to the SELL Process, let me suggest two weighty statements of affirmation that will reinforce your continued awareness. They provide suitable summary for our brief lesson on communication. Speak these firmly—out loud—to get your brain to accept them:

"I am constantly receiving messages."

To that I say heads-up, don't miss them! Stay alert when you are engaged in the SELL Process and be in your game. Never coast through communication on autopilot. Overcome filters. Recognize kinesics and make great effort to interpret them correctly as you carefully listen and observe.

"I am constantly sending out messages."

And to that statement I emphasize accepting *100 percent* responsibility for the messages you send. Yes, 100 percent. Oh, I have heard it said that communication is a two-way street. In theory, that is realistic since you cannot totally control the attitude or reaction of the other person. But this book is about *selling*! We are building on the premise that selling empowers you to skillfully alter the opinions of others and help them take mutually beneficial action. If you want to get the communication job done, you have to be the one to eloquently orchestrate your total message to reach your objective. Consider and perfect what you say and how you say it. Be aware of your tone and possible underlying messages such as condescension or intimidation. What might your non-verbals such as posture or minute facial clues transmit? Be very aware. Communication is a two-way street, but we pave the way and fill all of the chuckholes!

Clearly, the most important element of awareness in communication is *active listening*. Are you really listening intently versus merely hearing? Most of us do not listen well naturally, so it is essential to make a conscious mental effort to do it. Kick yourself if you let preoccupation, arrogance, prejudice, impatience, or just bad habits deter you from really listening to the other person. Listening— *active* listening—is imperative in selling. Active listening is a whole body, heart, and mind engagement with the other person. Your ears, eyes, mind, comments, and posture (kinesics) are focused on discovering what is in the other person's mind and heart. True needs and wants are what drive the other person's decisions, and the wise person is highly skilled at digging deep and recognizing these. Active listening must be done on purpose. Again, I underscore that you must decide to make a conscious mental effort to listen. It is a discipline that many struggle with, including me. I once had a mentor convict me to the core when he indicated that, "struggling is just *delayed obedience*." I finally accepted that I needed to shut my pie-hole and force myself to listen intently to the other person. The legendary Zig Ziglar once reminded an audience about the classic Bible story where Samson killed a thousand Philistines with the jawbone of an ass. He proceeded to say that, "Many sales are killed every day with the same weapon."

Due to the pivotal importance of listening to the whole of selling, the following list of listening disciplines is provided to help you get better. Please note that these are *disciplines* versus tips. Of course there is no comprehensive list that will automatically make you a better listener, but the following will help if you work daily to improve each item within your personal and business relationships.

Listening Disciplines:

Be sincere. If the other person picks up even the slightest clue that you are not real, the true disclosure stops.

Have an open mind. Delay judgment, and allow the other person to say even things you do not want to hear. Get the big picture. Don't jump to conclusions.

Be patient—allow completion. This goes with an open mind and requires you to bite your tongue, if needed. Sellers who have learned to count to 10 in their mind find that before they get through the count, astounding information surfaces. Utilize the "dead air" or those seemingly uncomfortable moments of silence in-between dialog to your advantage.

Do not interrupt. Avoid this temptation even if your interruption supports what they are saying. Enthusiasm is no excuse for this rude activity. If you have this habit, stop it.

Encourage more disclosure. This takes listening even a step further. After the person pauses, delay your points even more, and dig a little deeper.

Be alive. Give full attention. People tell you more when they feel that you want it and care. Stay alert and aware. Pick up their tone and kinesics. Let those key signals help give you the big picture and allow you to connect.

Be aware of your non-verbals. Emulate signals that solicit disclosure and draw out information. Maintain realistic eye contact. Make sure your aura creates a safe haven for other people to respond and open up. (Consider this suggestion to help you with this skill: get feedback from those who are close to you and include some honest introspection.) If your habitual non-verbals are intimidating, intense, judgmental, condescending, or visibly annoyed, you will not even get the chance to listen.

Be prepared. Preparation using the SELL Process allows you to focus on listening since your tactical plan has been documented.

Keep asking questions. This actually shows the other person that you care. People love to talk about themselves and what they do. Tap into this. People like listeners.

Take notes appropriately. This, of course, depends on the situation and may not apply in many selling interactions. In some cases it may be proper to ask permission. Yet it bears emphasis because it supports good listening so advantageously. When you take notes as someone talks, it shows interest and focus. It creates a consultative environment. It often encourages the other person to talk because it visually assures listening. Your notes provide reminders of key points and help keep you on track. They can even guide your summary when Locking action at the end! From a relationship-management standpoint, good records provide historical documentation. They also facilitate follow-up actions and fuel future interactions. The only downside that you need to figure out for yourself is how to take notes while maintaining adequate eye contact and still catching non-verbals. It *can* be done, and with practice you can adjust your method.

I usually scribble partial words or phrases and use arrows, circles, stars, and rough outlines that usually end up looking like a John Madden chalkboard. I fill in the blanks and often rewrite after the meeting, and I am good to go.

Limit your own talking. I like to suggest a rule of thumb when you go into the interaction—make it a goal to listen twice as much as you are speaking.

Catch and recover. Invariably you will slip and fail to listen as you should. You will. And when you do, catch yourself and learn to correct mid-stream. This is difficult and even embarrassing, but what a respectful and honoring way to demonstrate your desire to put aside your selfish propensity and *listen*.

Ingrain these disciplines into your daily interactions and understanding will begin to unfold. This leads to the next principle in asking great questions.

Bolster a desire to understand the other person.

Listening is the gateway to help us connect with and really understand other people. I personally think that one of the best things we can experience in this life is when someone really "gets" us and when we "get" them. If you never experience this level of understanding, life is a lonely journey. The SELL Process allows two people to really connect and understand one another. I have taught this to people who shared later that a personal SELL interaction ended up being one of the best connections they had ever experienced with a particular person. One lady who attended a sales training camp was not actually a salesperson with a territory and customer accounts. Her position was administrative, and due to her responsibilities with the sales team she was included in the training event. As I focused the customized event toward the sales team, the group was asked to choose a current deal they were working on and walk through the SELL Process Planning Tool for their next call with that selected target account. She asked me during a break what she should work on since she, of course, had no accounts. I asked her, "Do you have any situations where you are trying to get someone else to do something that you want them to do?" She immediately responded, "Yes, my daughter. She graduated from high school a year ago and she refuses to go to college. I hate to see her sit on her butt and drift when she has so much potential. We have had fight after fight on this subject." "There you go," I said. "Work on that as your target account." She proceeded to work very diligently on her SELL Process Planning Tool.

I received a call from her a few weeks later. "I closed my target account," she boasted. She proceeded to tell me that her interaction with her daughter was the deepest and most productive talk they had ever had! She choked back tears and continued, "I asked my prepared questions and instead of telling her what I wanted her to do, I just listened and made every effort to keep her sharing until I really understood." This mom was finally *selling* instead of *telling*. With trust built by mom's careful probing and patient listening, her daughter eventually shared the underlying truth that was precipitating the tension and fights. She reluctantly admitted to deep-rooted fears of leaving home, buried by layers of inferiority that made her feel like she would fail academically. Once good listening brought understanding, the mother was able to present her objective—to visit her own alma mater for a fun weekend to just check it out. The logical process paved the way for her to then show her daughter how college would benefit her and how it would be one of the most memorable periods in her life. Having a clear understanding of her daughter's specific fears, the mother was able to pinpoint encouragement and specific examples that proved her daughter had the academic ability to succeed. She Locked in a realistic action, and it was as easy as could be. No need to twist her arm or use the parental classic, "because I said so." Connecting with and understanding another person is why the SELL Process is so essential.

What does it mean to really understand someone? I suggest that it starts with humility. I visualize this by flipping the word "understand" around. To really understand someone else you must "stand under." There is a verse in Proverbs of the Bible that says: *"The purposes of a man's heart are deep waters, but a man of understanding draws them out."* Proverbs 20:5 NIV. If you take a servant knee, in a legitimate effort to honor what the other person truly thinks and feels, you end up winning in the end as well!

I mentioned earlier that I wished I could teach a foolproof technique for asking questions. I proceeded to explain that it is *less* about *technique*, and *more* about *dynamic human interaction.* I earnestly want you to grasp and possess this ability. I think stepping way back and getting a less pixellated view of this essential skill will do the trick. You see, asking questions in the Evaluate step is **less** about some things and **more** about other things.

It is **less** about *winging it*; although there is obviously an element of thinking and responding on your feet.

But it is **more** about the *personal discipline* required to prepare and execute well crafted questions. It is more about having the discipline to control your tendencies to talk, interrupt, finish, or even answer your own questions.

It is **less** about *control*; although you do gain control by asking questions. I have high respect for someone who can ask a well-placed question and almost covertly take control of the conversation.

But it is **more** about *responsiveness*. With your objective established and your questions documented and ready, you can more intently focus on listening and discovery, responding as an others-centered consultant.

It is **less** about *confirmation*; although you will typically confirm expected needs and anticipated outcomes.

But it is **more** about *discovery* as your inquisitive mind peels back layers of detail to find reality, which can surprisingly be more than you even hoped for.

It is **less** about the *lawyer style*; although your task may be building a solid case and winning over a desired verdict.

But it is **more** about the *doctor or servant style* in which your bedside manners and humble service foster trust to bring healing, even if it includes short-term pain.

It is **less** of a *science*; although rational thinking with the scientific method is woven into the process.

But it is **more** of an *art* in which you build on your creative gifts with tools of the trade and a heart that is passionately intense to make the perfect strokes. Masters develop a flair that utilizes certain processes and methodology, and deliver a masterpiece with artistic skill that cannot be articulated in a book.

Asking questions in the Evaluate step of the SELL Process is **less** about *you*;

and **more** about *THEM*.

It is up to you now to take this bigger perspective of the skill of asking questions and work hard on getting better and better. Asking questions as you listen alertly to understand can be perfected into an art if you are driven by a concerned, inquisitive mind.

Cultivate an inquisitive mind.

Earlier, as we learned about this step of the SELL Process, you drafted and perfected your questions. That pre-planning is the easy part. You cannot simply submit a few questions, get some surface answers, and jump right into the next step, presenting your answer, solution, or case, so to speak. In the interaction is where you must skillfully navigate through the dialog using your well-prepared questions as starting points to initiate trust and disclosure. You must stay exceptionally alert and incorporate all the disciplines of listening and understanding that we have been discussing.

When you ask a question and get some sort of response, ideally an inquisitive mind will intrinsically think, "Hmmm. I wonder what that means. I noticed a hesitation. What do I know about this? What do I not know? Who? Why?...?" Every question can lead to a host of questions. Cultivate that type of mindset in your selling. Little alert flags or pop-ups should be going off in your head as you touch on topics or issues that can conceal so much essential information. Now don't take it too far and antagonize the other person, relentlessly probing. Most err on the opposite extreme, so I am safe asking you to swing more to the side of probing, to help you make a decisive tactical correction.

Make it a rule to delay your judgments and hair-triggered solutions. It is so easy for a seller to pounce on certain words and charge right into what they wanted to say given the faintest hint of interest or weakness. I have literally watched salespeople biting at the bit to present what they have to offer, curtailing the Evaluation in a heartbeat. Some ask a question and then answer it! Some ask, impatiently tolerate the response, and seek the slightest gap in the conversation to dive into their offense. This is where offense takes on its secondary meaning—offensive.

In working with thousands to learn the SELL Process, this little piece of advice has been given many times: Dig deep! When the customer is opening up or spilling the beans, use reinforcing statements such as, "I see," "I agree," or "keep going" (but don't overdo it). Just create a safe environment that allows them to share. Try asking depth questions to get more detail like, "Help me understand what led to that," "You mentioned . . . tell me more," or "That is so important, could you elaborate?"

Your inquisitive mind and a discipline to ask well-crafted questions—digging deep, will protect you from entering a precarious place: "la la land." You see, if you are not extremely careful to uncover all the real facts and true decision criteria, there is a tendency to fantasize about the outcome. You dream of when the action will happen and talk your self into what might be happening behind the scenes. Instead you must qualify! Qualify early, often, and continuously.

Depending on your situation and your purpose for learning the SELL Process, this may be an occasional concern. For sales professionals who are interacting with customers all day, every day, qualifying is of utmost concern. (And Sales Managers everywhere are saying, "Thank you for putting that in this book.") I have had so many sales leaders who ask their people about calls recently made and they get responses that make you cringe. When the manager asks the salesperson, "When is this deal gonna happen?" the whimsical reply is, "I hope this month, cause I need it." And this one makes you really wonder what happened in the sales interaction: "Is this dude you took to lunch the decision maker?" and the reply, "I think so, he acts like it." Obviously, the tedious surgery of qualifying was omitted and I would bet that both of those calls were filled with presentation—rapid-fire presentations about products, services, and solutions. I call this, "drive-by selling." To put it bluntly, if you are spending your precious selling hours selling your brains out, doing demonstrations, writing detailed quotes with options, and perhaps driving all over the country, your potential customers better be qualified!

Ask the hard questions.

Here is a short list of qualifying questions that are imperative to uncover and confirm:

- Is there a need, desire or want?

- Do they perceive value like you do?

- Can and will they pay? What is their budget?

- Do you fit? Is this your market or niche? Do you even want this?

- Can you fulfill or deliver?

- Competition? Pricing?

- Is this person the decision-maker? What is their authority?

- What is the time frame for action?

- What is behind delays, politics, issues, emotional distance, etc.?

There are countless questions to ask, and it is an essential part of the SELL Process for you to ask them. If you make numerous calls on the same person or company in a longer selling cycle, be faithful to prepare appropriate wording and ask some of the qualifying questions above. Do this early in the cycle and often throughout each precious interaction. You will save yourself a lot of heartache and spinning of tires if you accept this responsibility and *qualify*.

Cultivating an inquisitive mind takes practice and discipline. Make it a personal goal to improve in the Evaluate step. Practice it daily at home and at work. You will be amazed at what you learn and how the exercise enhances and creates relationships. Never forget to, "ask more questions . . . and shut-up!"

Now you are ready to proceed to learning and preparing for the next step of the SELL Process: Leverage. Logically, after discovering the facts and desires, we can, with certainty, present an answer, solution, or appropriate action that matches. Showing how the other person will benefit is now possible and actually easy!

Chapter 5

Leverage—to match discovered desires with Benefits

Now in the very heart of the SELL Process, it is rightly time to do your thing. (Sorry. Half of you are now singing, "If you wanna see me do my thing, pull my string.") Seriously, moving into this step is a decisively timed thing. With selling discipline you won't easily get drawn into an early presentation of your case when someone inadvertently "pulls your string." In fact, from the obvious preeminence of the previous chapter you now understand that a so-called presentation is not a stand-alone activity of selling. We don't just state our case or demonstrate our product and politely leave, to wait by the phone for a call. Of course, presentation is expected and necessary, but *timing* is everything! I recommend holding off on your points as long as realistically feasible. A common phrase in classic sales lingo promoted the idea that you need to have a "sales pitch." Now you know that selling is a whole lot more about *catching* than it is *pitching!*

This step includes your Leverage. By definition leverage is *the power to influence a person or situation to achieve a particular outcome.* Leverage can run the spectrum because of the host of possible selling situations that may be faced. Sometimes Leverage includes a logical answer, solution, recommendation, or corrective action. In other cases it might entail presenting technical details or formal specifications and could include audio-visual or hands-on demonstrations or presentations. Nearly all marketplace-type selling involves selling your product and/or service, and selling your company added value and/or you. Persuasive skill and the ability to articulate product and value enthusiastically is a big part of becoming a sales professional. Just a side note: Product or application training in any commerce selling function is a cornerstone. Just don't follow the patterns of so many organizations who treat that as the entire game plan for selling, overlooking selling skills and the *process* that is indeed the vehicle. (I now step down from my soapbox.)

Hence, a broad range of things could be included in the Leverage step.

In *all* situations the essential component involves *Benefits!*

Benefits with a capital B

Have you ever heard of the classic terms *features and benefits*? Some readers who are career salespeople may have had this concept, and specific applications of its use, drilled into their heads. Admittedly, *features and benefits* are the *blocking and tackling* of sales. The skill of Benefit selling is a primary fundamental of selling, but it is not quite as easy as it might seem on the surface. I guess you could say it is easy on the chalkboard—hard on the field. With the wealth of training that most professional salespeople receive from their internal sources such as manufacturers, engineering teams, marketing departments, etc., one would think that the majority would be pretty good at doing this. I have clearly observed otherwise. Evidently, even systematic training with detailed lists and brochures filled with F&Bs (as so called) lacks the impetus to equip salespeople to actually convey them effectively to another person in a dialog.

To get a workable understanding of the mechanics of Benefit selling, let me break it down. Benefits stem from features. A feature is a trait or an element of your product, service, company, or proposed solution. A feature might be some difference or uniqueness that your offering provides which has the potential to benefit the other person or allow them to gain. Simply, a feature is what your product, solution, or company *looks like*. It is what the product or service *does*. I am defining this broadly because I do not want to limit this concept to the common understanding of "features on a new car." Granted, cruise control or alloy wheels are features by definition. But, in any selling interaction it is important to consider the features of the thing or action you are attempting to persuade the other person to accept. What does it look like and what will it do? Those elements of your objective are features.

So you have identified the features, now what? It is essential that you articulate how the person you are selling to Benefits. Just voicing or implying some notable features is not enough. Worse yet, rattling off every possible feature you can think of and hoping one hits the mark is not a good method either. I call this "machine gun selling." *Say it, spray it, and pray it works*—doesn't work. Never assume that the other person will make that connection as to how they Benefit. Part of our selling job is to help them perceive the advantages and thus be internally motivated to action on our objective! Actually, this is assured by asking such good questions in the Evaluate step and listening so well, that you can survey all of the possible features and zero in on the features that really matter to this particular person. Somehow a connection must be made as to what each selected feature means to the person you are selling to. How do they Benefit from the product, service, or action that you are putting forward?

To help make this connection, consider tentative or typical benefits. A typical benefit is a possible advantage. These are benefits that you project which logically apply to most people—generic benefits. Often, there are many typical benefits for each feature, if you put enough thought into thinking them up. This is the stratum of benefits found in most brochures or marketing literature. Unfortunately, this level of benefit selling is where most sellers stop.

Benefit selling is not a regurgitation of undeniable facts that you have learned somewhere. To manufacturers, I respectfully offer this insight after years of teaching selling skills. My 22-year background in the factory and in industrial sales has confirmed to me the fact that literature cannot really sell Benefits. Literature is a form of information; it is not communication. Dropping literature off would be like doctors dropping off scalpels—only good in the hands of the surgeon. The ability to sell Benefits is an exclusive skill that must be done by *people* who know how to sell—people who understand the SELL Process. After Starting the interaction in a way that attracts the other person and begins the dialog, questions should be asked to discover true needs and wants. Then, and only then, the seller can relate Benefits to the other person. Specific Benefits for the other person are what create Leverage and tip the scale to your favor!

Effective feature and benefit selling involves conveying Benefits with a capital B. To accomplish this requires thought before the interaction in which you anticipate the possible hot buttons or core motivators that might spawn the desired action. During the SELL Process interaction you carefully Evaluate in step two, digging deep and staying alert to discover what is important to the other person. Benefits are unique to each person. Each individual's personality style and how they view the world impacts their perception of Benefits. And when you reveal these and effectively substantiate them, the result is Leverage—influence to tip the scale in favor of your objective!

For the most part, your Leverage step is relatively easy once you have become proficient with your particular offering, whether it be product, service, system, solution, agreement, or whatever the case may be. Granted, you need to know your stuff. That becomes your academic responsibility. Once you have that knowledge, the execution depends first on your effectiveness in step two and then rests on how persuasively and enthusiastically you can match discovered desires with how this particular person, in this particular situation, **B**enefits (with a capital B).

Again, no matter what type of selling interactions you are reading this book to improve upon, the overriding concept is to relate your Leverage dialog so that it undeniably exposes to the other person *how **they** will Benefit!*

Motivators and emotion

Primarily, Benefits are rooted in the thing or things that motivate a particular individual. As you begin to understand Benefits it will really help to consider motivators and emotion. Human beings are complex and I am not attempting to veer off into the fields of psychology and behavior. Yet, for the sake of seeing how these things play into the SELL Process, and Leverage in particular, I will highlight some things. Below is a list of some possible motivators:

- Profit, cost savings, money gain
- Convenience
- Security, safety
- Personal pride
- Comfort
- Envy, competitive drive
- Fear, worry, stress

- Selfish drives for advancement, acclaim, sex, or validation

- Tastes, values

- Erratic emotion, inappropriate determinations

As you review this condensed list, keep in mind that the obvious ones are not always the deep-rooted motivation for some people. People are complicated and some can even be goofy or idiosyncratic. For example, at first glance a person might seem to be motivated by profit, cost savings, or money gain. With evaluation and keen observation, you might interpolate that the *real* motivation is personal pride or a need to validate themselves. Maybe they need to save money to look good in front of a boss or solely out of fear. We could camp out on this subject indefinitely, but I think you get the point. People Benefit based on their own individual reasons, whatever they might be.

Emotion also plays into someone taking action, big time! Granted, every person you deal with may not be emotional, per se. They may in fact be very reserved and stoic. But believe me, every human being does what they decide to do for a reason—and it is based on how they *feel* about it. I found the background of this word to be very interesting. The English word is based on the Latin word *emovere*, where *e-* means "out" and *movere* means "move." Emotion essentially means to move or be moved. We often say that a philanthropist, for example, was *moved* emotionally and therefore donated a large sum of money to a charity. In response to being emotionally *moved* by the loss of a friend, a rock star might give a benefit concert.

The related term *motivation* is also derived from the word *movere*. Our task in planning is to think of ways to utilize the customer's motivators and emotion and creatively channel them to the desired action or objective.

Enthusiasm

Here is where enthusiasm is your ingredient of choice. One veteran salesperson called enthusiasm "knowledge on fire." Other people will only get as excited about what you have to say as you are. Enthusiasm is contagious. Believe in yourself. If you are selling a product or representing a company, how much you believe in those things will go a long way in enhancing even a standard presentation.

Enthusiasm, having the root word *theos,* meaning *god*, was ancient Greek, meaning originally, *god in you*. After some thought, the symbolism of this portrays a great picture. People are looking for answers. They are in need of someone who has wisdom and authority. They feel safe when dealing with someone who is confident—not a deceiver, but someone who has a big-picture perspective and embraces truth. Be the answer to their prayers!

Pre-planning for the Leverage step begins with perhaps white paper, and by all means should not be limited to a small box on your SELL Process Planning sheet. You might use that space for outline notes or reminders on key points as a cheat sheet of sorts. Some selling situations may require extensive preparation and sales or marketing support tools for this step.

If you sell a product, you would of course, include

features of that product. Likewise you would include particular features for a *service* you might provide. In some cases, you may be providing a commodity or near commodity. Just remember that the closer your product or service looks like your competitors—the better your selling skill has to be!

You may be selling a premium solution that is notably better, yet much more expensive than other options. Perhaps what you offer provides documentable or intangible Benefits that far outweigh the initial price. If that is the case, your Leverage step better make that clear.

Price is what customers think about . . . when the salesperson gives them nothing else to think about!

I have no quarrel when a competitor has a lower price. They know better than anyone what their product or service is worth!

In the majority of marketplace selling, you would also want to include the value factors of your organization—your value proposition or unique differences. This is very important to Leverage if all else, such as product or service, is level ground with competitors. Why you? Why should this other person do business with you? If you do not know the answer to that question—*who does*? Remember: the one thing the competition does not have is *you*. Sell yourself and your company.

If you are planning for an interaction with a superior, subordinate, friend, or partner, you might simply articulate the points of your solution or idea. Sell your proposed plan of action or state your case succinctly.

But again, in every case, your Leverage discourse must

include how the other person will gain or Benefit! I've seen it delivered in everything from formal presentations to spontaneous shots that were sort of staccato in nature. The Leverage step is not always a big chunk of your presentation after a grueling Evaluate step. Often, it can flow back and forth naturally between steps, nailing down Benefits after each discovered need. Are you seeing what I meant when I said you can *get game*? No matter how the process transpires, perceived Benefits are what fuel the fire and pave the way for the next step: Lock!

It may have already occurred to you that pre-planning this step conflicts a bit with what I have been preaching for two chapters; you can't do step three until you first ask questions in step two. And at this point you haven't had the interaction! For planning purposes, all you are trying to do is create your Leverage content and *anticipate the hot buttons.* If you labor over your preparation enough to answer the overriding question, "What does this mean to *this* person and how will *they* gain?" then you will have greased the path in your mind to, in the interaction, adapt and highlight the discovered hot buttons, related as Benefits to the other person.

Apply the Process

 Now insert your bookmark and get to work on your tactical plan for this Leverage step.

Chapter 6

Lock—to confirm conviction and agree to action

We are on the last lap! (For some reason I hear Lloyd in the movie *Dumb and Dumber* saying with relief, "We're there!") This final step is the bottom line of the SELL Process. If, after doing all the other steps of the process well, you don't Lock action or results, then the effort was in vain. Get to the center of the target and finish the deal. Do not leave things hanging or wishy-washy. For some of you, completion of this step is how you get paid!

Stay positive!

From the inception of your objective in your pre-planning and throughout the design and execution of each step, the Lock has been your target. Keep that positive attitude! It always helps to picture a positive outcome in your mind. Remember: this process is good for the other person too! Your plan is designed carefully to assure a both-win outcome. Sure, I realize that anything could happen and the simple exercise of thinking positively about the situation will not guarantee results. But I will say this: negative thinking has a horrendous way of turning into a self-fulfilling prophecy. It seems that people who think the worst or go into the SELL Process expecting to fail, many times, do not even see a potential opportunity when it presents itself in the dialog. I have watched this happen in actual sales calls.

Sometimes everyday events paint a picture. One time, when my kids were little, we were at my youngest son's youth soccer tournament. This was a big game. The team had to win in order to advance to the next round. The score was tied and we were in the final period with less than a minute remaining. In a dramatic steal, the ball was controlled by our team's little superstar, the coach's son, of course. (He never sits the bench, but that is another issue altogether.) Anyway, the sidelines went bonkers as he skillfully navigated past each defender's frantic attempt to stop him in time. One mom was crying. One dad was actually easing onto the playing field, captivated. And then the shot . . .

. . . right smack into the hands of the dreaded twerp of a goalie, dressed in a brightly colored jersey, so big on the little guy it looked like a dress. And it was over. The mom was still crying. The dad started yelling at one of the refs. What happened? The talented little athlete, as good as he was, allowed himself to get fixated on the negative, the twerp. And where he focused, the rest of him seemed to just follow merrily along.

Coach Lombardi put it this way, "A team that thinks it's going to lose—is going to lose."

There may be quite a few of you who are trying to stay positive but you feel very uncomfortable being assertive, and you seem to feel a reluctance to Lock in action with someone. This is understandable, especially when you learn that, just as some people are very task-oriented and assertive, others are more people-oriented or tend to be more compliant and focused on relationships. This is fine. No one style is good or bad. How you value doing business and the way you are wired is beautiful, whatever that looks like. However, keep in mind that we are *selling*. That means that in this process, our mission is to adapt the interaction to the other person, allowing improved interactions and a more harmonious relationship. Flexibility is the key. Therefore, your level of assertiveness is more dependent on helping the other person achieve an objective that will benefit them, and adjusting your own style to better match how they might like to get things done. If your inner self feels uncomfortable, that is not always a true indication that Locking it in was too aggressive. If this describes you, start stretching your comfort level. Especially if your job is being a salesperson! Staying back too far from "crossing the line" can lose you and your organization a lot of money. It is OK to step your toe right up to that line. Give it a try. If the other person balks, step back. Then you will know right where you are and that you gave it your best effort. (When we get into the SELL defense chapter it will help you immensely.)

I think it's important to note that there are some prevailing negative stigmas about selling in general that reinforce reluctance. Many mainstream movies have depicted the sales occupation as a brood of deceitful connivers. If you have watched the salesroom scene in Glengarry Glen Ross, you know what I mean. Alec Baldwin screamed, "A-B-C. A-Always, B-Be, C-Closing. Always be closing, always be closing," and pressured the stunned sales team to close, "'Cause only one thing counts in this world: get them to sign on the line which is dotted." And who hasn't had some life experience where a salesperson tricked us or played a game with us? No doubt, some have endured a pathetic sales hell where high-pressure tactics were employed and you escaped, livid. I have. And I still get ticked when I recount it. These fragments haunt the noble and vital profession of selling. The SELL Process is the antithesis of these methods and together we will change the image of what selling really is.

There are even detrimental connotations surrounding the common sales term: "close." I accept the fact that this term has been around for a long time and it may remain a part of some salespeople's language, but it supports some negative images. "Close" implies the end, or shutting of a door. Actually, in good selling, we are opening the door or opening an opportunity. It is the beginning of a relationship, not the end.

Thankfully, the profession of selling has progressed beyond the old school method of: *get in, sell, get out.* Granted, there are selling environments where the cycle is short and selling interactions are do or die, but consultative selling interaction has become the method of choice. In our service revolution, and the predominant pattern of long-term partnerships and single-source purchasing, consultative selling has become the norm.

Locking is logical

The Lock step is logical. If you have kept the SELL Process in harmony with their process, Locking in action or agreement is effortless. In fact, if you have to twist their arm or feel like you need to push, you probably did something wrong or missed something in one of the first three steps! You have reached the center of the target and it should be as natural as a gentle tap of the finger to tip the scale.

Don't get me wrong—you still have to ask. Some tend to make it a rule to "let the other person close themselves." This is a fine outcome and with the process you are learning it is probable, but never rule out the responsibility that either way, you must Lock action.

I received a call from a sales manager after he heard me speak at a convention asking if I would come and do a workshop at his company's annual sales meeting. "My people are weaklings," he said. "I need you to *teach my people to close!*" My reply was a bit hesitant as I indicated that I really don't take that approach. I suggested that if I came in with that mindset we run the risk of forcing them to the other extreme and they may get the message that selling involves pressure and manipulation techniques. He needed results and a determined drive built into his professionals. We opted to teach them the SELL Process and it accomplished precisely what he intended from the onset.

This step says it all—*Lock to confirm conviction and agree to action.* Each word in that phrase helps you grasp the concept. Confirm is actually two Latin words, *con*: together, and *firm*: to strengthen. I like the idea here; it means to *strengthen* **together**. If they have been shown how they Benefit and are now convicted in their own heart to do the action, agreeing is a mutual thing that you strengthen by Locking a specific action. It may be a purchase order. It may be a date that is set. It can, in some cases, be simply a verbal acceptance. But you agree together on an action.

Buying signals

Ironically, people usually give you a signal when they are ready. Sadly, even experienced salespeople can miss these indiscriminate "buying signals" if they are not attentive. It is easy when you are off to the races in your Leverage step to oversell or enjoy that part a little too much, missing the clue to finish!

If the other person asks an action question like "Are you sure?" or "Do you have these in stock?" *Ding, ding, ding . . .* ASK for the action!

Perhaps they make a positive comment like, "Mmm . . . that is great!" or "We have needed to do this for awhile." *Ding, ding, ding . . .* ASK for the action!

Sometimes a person might just light up non-verbally and nod their head or express interest with their face or eyes. Yup. *Ding, ding, ding . . .* ASK for the action!

Ask!

You must ask! Don't assume that they will suggest action on their own, as we already admitted could easily happen. The way I see it, selling is your job and usually they are expecting *you* to Lock it in. There has even been a few times where I thought it might be a bit premature to ask and they just responded to my Lock with, "Yes. I'm tired of having this on my plate. Let's do this." I was as shocked as Tommy Boy (in the movie of the same name) when his first customer said yes to buying brake pads! It's been said, "You miss every shot you don't take." Ask early and often. Some studies have indicated that in typical selling markets, five to seven requests to act are average. I am not proposing pit bull like aggression, but appropriate trial Locks throughout the interaction are a natural part of the process. As you may recall, the SELL Process is not necessarily step-by-step. Selling is very dynamic. Trial Locking is your friend.

When you trial Lock after making a point, it finds out the other person's opinion. It may lead you back to step two, asking more questions to really understand how they look at the issue at hand. Trial Locking is effective at surfacing true objections. Following an eloquent answer to a voiced objection with a Lock is one sure way to surface the *real* issue if the initial balk was a smokescreen. Locking also qualifies the decision-making authority of the person you are interacting with. If they have alluded to having the power all along, you can find out real quickly if that is totally true by Locking. "Well . . . tell ya what . . . um, let me run this by the big boys and I might shake some money loose", is representative of a decision-maker wannabe. Trial

Locking provided you insight as to what your challenge might be. Don't settle for that response. In this instance, a quick recoil back to the Evaluate step should be your gut reaction. If you need to gauge how hot or cold this person really is to your objective, trial Lock! Are we getting close to the end? Trial Lock. Actually, a reasonable amount of trial Locking keeps the interaction length under control and the best thing is—they just might say "YES!"

Now, if they don't say yes, what might that mean? It could indicate that your Start hit a brick wall and you never really attracted them to the objective. They may be confused or overwhelmed. You might need to throw out another line. Many times there just needs to be more questions asked, so further probing in the Evaluate step is in order. Sometimes the other person may not quite accept or even perceive the Benefits you presented, and it may take more Leverage to sway them. In any case, be carefully persistent. Tenacity is essential on the uncertain sea of selling. It can take quite a few "No" responses to get to that glorious "Yes!" (Just know when to cut your losses and walk. And there is a time for that. Your call.)

This discussion on dealing with negative responses leads us right into the other essential part of your tactical selling—SELL Defense. You can plan out your offense before you enter the interaction, and that is vital. Invariably, however, you will be jolted into your defense. Objections, complaints, and negotiation ploys are looming in most interactions. Help is on the way! We will equip you for your SELL Defense in the next chapter.

Delays and stalls

At this juncture I want to address one adversarial situation that is common when Locking. How do we deal with delays and stalls? These can definitely be legitimate but can just as easily be evasion. You need to determine which. After you learn how to do your SELL Defense you will treat and handle this just like you would an objection. So keep that in mind. For now I implore you not to just accept the delay and agree on a future time frame. Of course, if the situation has a genuinely required delay, your Lock would be to specifically nail down a proactive timetable or date to take incremental action. Even if it reeks of going sour, you need to try to stay in the loop or jockey for a better position. Mark you calendar and keep your hope alive. Things change and people change positions. And I would add for career salespeople, in the meantime, get out there and prospect to get some more irons in the fire!

When a delay is casually mentioned, my internal reaction is usually an emotional tanking. I have learned to maintain composure and control my non-verbal reaction of disappointment or frustration. Don't roll over or just give up. Swing back to selling. Ask the hard questions. Be creative and resourceful by repackaging your solution or proposal if you can—if that would help (without making needless concessions.) As a last resort, to be used in moderation, it might help to ask, *What will it take to move now? What is really in the way?* Or even, *What should I do to make this happen?*

Please don't forget that there is a good side to delays. Requests for delays often mask immediate opportunities.

I have discovered from experience that a good majority of stalls or delays are merely knee-jerk reactions by the other person to defer for surprising reasons! I'm sure you have dealt with individuals that were so stinking busy they were gun-shy to accept even obviously advantageous deals at the first go around. If you cater to their tired, sometimes selfish, attempt at dodging the activity they will gladly let you. But if you want to serve them well, keep selling. Offering some creative legwork on your part often does the trick—and the frantic mood they live in actually facilitates an equally fast decision: "OK, let's do it. Take it from here, I have other fish to fry." Often, busy companies and people have money flowing, and they are quick to buy *convenience.*

When you finally go for it and ask for the action, commitment, or order—Shut-up! Don't speak another word until you get a response. There is such power in silence. Your legs might be shaking, and your neck may be twitching forward, but hold the fort. As uncomfortable as the silence feels, speaking up again is worse. If you ask for a commitment or action and the person stares at you like a deer in the headlights, it may seem like an eternity. But wait . . .

Wait . . .

Keep waiting . . .

If you yield to the temptation and blurt out something else, you take them off the hook! The pressure to share information that may have been necessary, yet tough to disclose, is relieved—and you may never find out what was about to be said. In some instances your additional talk may distract their thought process. They were deciding and then got skipped off the track.

Your SELL job is complete. Let it happen.

Oh, and a tip here from my negotiation course. *Nearly every time* a seller adds a comment or tag line after they just Locked . . . it ends up being a concession!

Locking techniques

Are you ready now to pre-plan your Lock? It might be the easiest step of the SELL Process to prepare. Base it on your objective and write it in words that work for you and fit the situation at hand. Before you pick up the pencil and put in your bookmark one more time, I would like to offer some Locking techniques. These are *never* intended for use as manipulation or deceit! They just provide techniques to make it easier for you to do what must be done to finalize the action. Make it comfortable and natural. When you Lock or secure a mutual agreement, BOTH win!

Here are some techniques that can assist you in Locking action:

Assume Acceptance Lock—Just move forward as if it is a done deal and if they don't nix it, you just Locked naturally.

Instruction Lock—These are nice. You just say, "Here's what you need to do . . ." or "First I will . . . and then we . . ."

Minor Decision Lock—Asking the person to decide on a related point can confirm that it is truly *go time*. "Do you want this on Tuesday or is Friday better?" Asking for decisions on options, color, quantity, extras, etc. is a non-threatening way to verify acceptance.

Closed-Ended Question Lock—Ask directly and wait. Don't you dare say another word!

Summarizing Lock—Point by point, summarize the agreed upon Benefits you discussed and remind them of the value they will receive. This Lock respects that they might not be as familiar with the points that you made as you are. For you they may be memorized or embedded into your head. Listing on paper to provide a visual is helpful as long as you don't start looking like they are a victim of a canned methodology. Also, this Lock can help avoid the phenomenon called "buyers remorse."

Testimonial Lock—Referencing a similar, respected person who took this same action successfully, might be the play that pushes them over any hindrance.

Puppy Dog Lock—Hey, if it works for Starts why couldn't it work for Locks? Mercy orders still pay the bills. Getting action simply because you are cute works too.

Contract Lock—This is a given for much commerce selling. Complete and sign an appropriate document. You might use a standard agreement or even financing and credit approval papers.

Payment Lock—This is also for commerce. Ask for a purchase order (P.O.) or even the classic "cash or charge." Discussing payment terms can facilitate the Lock.

Special Price or Limit Lock—If a limited supply, timeframe, or a special price is true, this can be the incentive to "act today." Just be careful not to sound pushy or use it with a person who hates pressure.

One more important hint before you write out your Lock. Keep the positive momentum. Make sure you don't accidentally water down your Lock by "back-door" phraseology. If you need to get a positive response, or if your job demands that you get sales results, don't drive to the basket and wimp out by missing the slam-dunk. Here are a few classic examples to help expose this tendency:

> *"Are there any other issues or hesitations to doing this?"*
> Why fish for an objection? This implies low confidence or a history of rejections. It plants the subliminal thought in the other person's mind to try and think up a possible reason to say no.

> *"I sorta think perhaps this might be better unless you are committed to the other option."*
> Kill me now.

And please don't butcher a noble attempt for "add-on" or what is termed as "suggestion selling" by pulling one like this: *"You don't want to double the order, do you?"* Positive wording is so much better.

This or any positive variation will work: *"You buy this consistently. I can double the order and save you a few bucks in the long run."*

Again, the beauty of writing it out ahead is that you can prevent some of these previously unnoticed pitfalls and put ongoing effort into changing your habitual wording patterns.

Apply the process

 After considering some possible techniques that might fit for your target situation, fill out the last section of your SELL Process Planning Tool.

You did it! Now you have learned the SELL Process and how to effectively prepare your offense before you engage in any selling interaction. Selling is a dynamic, on-your-feet process and your instincts and flexibility will improve by sticking with the ongoing discipline of preparation before each sales call or important meeting. Over time you can become highly skilled at selling. Training and practice are what it takes to keep getting better!

In the final chapter we will take a hard look at how you can build on this foundation and achieve a small margin of excellence, which produces a huge reward!

Now that you have worked through the last four chapters, working on your target situation, you are just about ready to conduct your first interaction using the SELL Process. You will be amazed at how well you do! Once you feel how much better you run the interaction and how much more confident, focused, and connected you are—you will be a believer in the SELL Process and the discipline of preparation before the interaction! You have your offense ready. But hang on for one more essential chapter of learning.

Let's work on our SELL Defense.

Chapter 7

SELL Defense: how to handle objections, complaints and ploys

Get ready. At some point, anywhere in the interaction (which you had all beautifully planned out) an objection to what you are selling may loom. An objection may smack you in the face as soon as you Start. Some resistance may build as you go for the Lock or lead toward asking for action. Some may pop up right when you hit your stride and knock you out of kilter. You might even ask a great question and get a completely unrelated confrontation in reply.

When you are jolted into your defense please do not be surprised or disappointed. Our goal in learning SELL Defense is to help you become comfortable with the uncomfortable. The process of selling and productive interaction in general, usually involves a level of healthy stress. If that puzzles you, please understand that *all* stress or tension is not bad. There is some level of tension in every action or change. It usually does not feel good at the time, however it is necessary for all of us when changing course or making decisions. Good stress is normal and can be healthy if managed. Stress is on a continuum. At one end of the spectrum you may have absolutely no pressure, discomfort, or stress which obviously results in little or no productive change. Heating it up to the other extreme of the spectrum results in destructive blow-ups and emotional havoc. Wisdom is managing stress to the optimal level, which comes with thoughtful anticipation, experience in the process, and a "heads-up" awareness. This varies with every situation and the individuals involved, so it behooves the seller to learn good defense and handle it like a pro.

With the possibility of negative territory ahead, an attitude check is in order. Even though talk of tension, defense, offense, and overcoming objections seems adversarial—and has that potential—you must make provision to maintain positive control. Resist, and keep resisting the mindset of "winners and losers." Truly, the premise of selling that we learned from the first words of this book has been that our job is to create and orchestrate a both-win scenario. Notice I was careful to use the term "both-win" versus the idiom "win-win." I admit that some people and some buyers think that a win-win is when they win twice! Yes, some people will be rough and some even relentless or downright mean. But this is not a conquest. Selling is all about cooperation through inter*action*. If roadblocks exist you must expose them and deal with them. Then you need to swing back to selling, learn precisely what the real situation is, and somehow help them to change their thinking.

Objections equal opportunities

If an objection is tucked away somewhere, creating doubts, apprehension, or underlying termination of the objective, the best thing that could happen is to get it out in the open. Only then will you be capable of addressing it and eliminating it. Objections equal opportunities! When you look at this realistically, an objection by the other person actually indicates that they have a level of interest and are willing to engage. At least they are willing to interact and discuss the issue at hand. I would worry if they have concerns but *don't* object! Objections can be clues to their hot buttons and this attempt to voice it and risk additional dialog indicates the importance of this matter from their perspective. One interpretation might be, "Fix this . . . and I'll move forward." So proceed into the challenge of responding to objections with confident resolve and embrace them. Objections can be your platform to show how good you are and how skillfully you can win the other person over. I am not condoning a response like jumping up with both index fingers pointing at the person with a resounding, "I'm glad you asked!" But picture your response sort of like the stride of a PGA tour golfer who has played 17 holes brilliantly—needing only a few well struck balls to par the 18th, defend their first place position on the leader board, and secure the jacket—unshaken and actually excited to do what he knows he can do if he keeps his focus. As a sales professional, become a master of the selling process.

The natural response

So how can you proceed to that level of selling? It takes work, but you will be delighted when you learn how basic and fundamental SELL Defense is. As a starting point, let's identify the *natural* response to objections, complaints, negotiation ploys, or really any remark during an interaction that puts you on the spot.

The natural response results in an immediate answer. This is especially tempting if you have a holster full of good answers! Veterans and technical gurus are most apt to naturally come back with what seems to be a sure-fire prescription. But let me state this as clearly and firmly as possible: do NOT respond immediately with your answer or rebuttal! Please accept that and burn it into your brain. Do not come flying back with an answer. Shortly, I will explain the simple, trained methodology used to handle objections. For now, understand that a "fight" response is one of the natural responses that should be trained and conditioned out of your defense. Natural tendencies when put on the spot with negative retorts include **Fight**, **Flight** or **Freak**. I give those responses straight Fs.

When your reaction is to *fight*, it may send a message that you hear this opposition all the time, and you are half-cocked and ready to shoot. It may even sound to the other person that you did not even listen or process what they just said, retorting instinctively. A fight response is natural for some personalities, yet it ends up being so combative. Fight responses include arguing, taking things personally, blaming others, making excuses, and trying to justify self. Fighting may be a natural, adrenal response, but in selling relationships it is far less effective than it might be in the wild, with Bear Grylls so to speak. Dale Carnegie, in the classic how-to book *How to Win Friends and Influence People* reminded us that, "You can't win an argument, because if you lose, you lose it; and if you win it, you lose it." You may even lose the relationship.

Some people react to objections in a completely opposite fashion—avoiding, ignoring, side-stepping, fantasizing, or not even dealing with the issue at hand. This natural *flight* response denies resolution and sets up a pattern of ineffectiveness, often with tons of *reasons* (but few plausible *excuses*). If a person refuses to come out of this cave of conflict fear, it can become like heliophobia, an irrational fear of the sun. Face and even embrace the butterflies in your gut. Unchecked, the growth of pending fear can result in the third natural response, to *freak*!

I've seen this third response firsthand. Someone gets put on the spot in an interaction that was moving along at a pretty good clip and BOOM! "Well, um...um...whew... um???. . . %#@" is the only thing that comes to mind. Underarms drip, tongue thickens, mouth gets dry, and you get a dangerous freak on. Pet phrases like, "to tell you the truth" can gush out. Ticks and poker tells are the outcomes of visible nervousness. I can't help but visualize the classic scene in Tommy Boy where Chris Farley sits in the diner and explains, as he pulverizes his dinner roll: *"Let's say I go into some guy's office. Let's say he's even remotely interested in buying something. Well, then I get all excited like Jojo, the idiot circus boy, with a pretty new pet. The pet is my possible sale. Oh, my pretty little pet, I love you. So, I stroke it and I pet it and I massage it. Hee hee, I love it. I love my little naughty pet. You're naughty! Then I take my naughty pet and go squish! Aah! I killed it. I killed my sale. That's when I blow it."*

Fight, Flight, or Freak—natural responses that naturally shut down the selling process.

There is a better way—the *trained* response. You can learn to act . . . not react!

The trained response

Be pragmatic enough to understand that it is very difficult to change a response pattern that may be deeply seated. It will take dedication and tenacious effort. As simple or minor as the corrective actions might appear, be ready to drill SELL Defense in until it becomes embedded into your cerebrum.

The lionized Vince Lombardi, made this statement: "The most important thing a coach needs is knowledge that his team can or can't play under pressure." Yogi Berra said something like, "Half this game is 95% mental!" You have to govern the pressure and win the head game first. This is done with a trained response that is **Poised**, **Professional**, and **Practiced**. (Straight P's for Passing grades versus the F's!)

Wouldn't it be great to be *poised* in these negative situations—gentle, confident, relaxed, steady, yet firm? *Professional* interaction is others-centered, empathetic (not pathetic), and logical. Cooperation through interaction can become almost effortless! A pre-planning regimen facilitates perfected wording, smooth tone, and powerful delivery. Of course, being well-*practiced* is the requirement to assure that you are ready. This allows you to clearly articulate Benefits for the other person and ultimately Lock action!

Let's walk through our defense now and then let the training and practice begin.

Anticipate objections

Foresight and preparation will minimize the times you are caught off guard and subsequently slip down old ruts of those deadly natural responses. Before any interaction, survey the potential hazards. Take a few moments to consider possible objections that you anticipate for the pending situation.

It helps to do research or gather some insider information on the individual or organization involved. Look online at websites and check social media. Talk to other vendors or people connected to them. Team sharing is a notable resource. Other team members may know this person or may have faced a similar situation, so they can help.

This data can directly correlate to potential objections and should be routine contemplation. Sales teams can gain a further advantage by studying the competition and getting a handle on relative strengths and weaknesses.

Sales Professionals or sales teams often hear many of the same objections over and over. There may be a myriad of variations on the themes but quite often salespeople or teams can zero in on a pretty comprehensive list of the major objections faced. By all means this list can be specific to the industry, current conditions, recent changes etc.

Some examples might be:

"Your price is too high!" (The mother of all sales objections)

"We're happy with our current provider."

"Your company blew its chance."

"I don't have a budget for this."

"Your manager is a jerk!"

"Too late. Where were you before?"

I think what Vince Lombardi said applies here: "There are only five or six big plays in every game and you have to make them to win. In a time of crisis, it is absolutely imperative."

 If you are a career sales professional, or are part of a team of reps, put your bookmark in this page and invest some time in listing these prototypical objections now. If you are applying this to an upcoming situation, brainstorm possible objections that could rear their ugly heads in the interaction.

Why do people object?

Now, it should be carefully considered: *why* do customers and those we interact with object? Think on that for a moment.

Granted, an objection might be a legitimate complaint or concern. But the same words, sounding essentially the same way, on the other hand might be a negotiation ploy designed to unearth a concession or gain the upper hand in a dialog. Which one? You cannot know at face value. Some objections might be a way to test your ability or resolve. There are some people and some in the purchasing profession that have actually adopted a confrontational style. They yell, and it works for them. I'm sure you know the type. Often objections are merely cries for more information or clarification. Perhaps your contact has been lied to by others and has misinformation. Who knows if someone badmouthed you beforehand and skewed his or her view of you. Don't rule out that they may just be confused, distracted, or making excuses to get rid of you.

Again, this solidifies the proposition that when someone objects or puts you on the spot in any way—DO NOT respond immediately with your answer or rebuttal. Oh yes, we agreed that you need to have answers ready, but your trained response must follow a proven methodology. Here is the good news about SELL Defense:

The same SELL Process used for pre-planning of your *offense* can be used as a methodology for preparing and responding to objections—your *defense*!

In selling interactions, the best defense is a good offense! Swing back to selling!

SELL Defense Response Tool

I also provide a SELL template for documenting your defense preparation. You can download a SELL Defense Response Tool—go to:

www.salesprofessionaltraining.com/selltools

This tool has a very similar framework as your SELL Offense and can serve as a worksheet to log each anticipated objection and develop a persuasive response on each sheet.

Remember: in selling your best defense is a good offense. When an objection comes your way, SELL!

Perhaps you are thinking, "But how do I get back on the offense? I just got stung. My heart is pounding. I inhaled and clinched mid-breath as my brain is scrambling."

Boy, you are gonna love this: Your key defensive maneuver is very simple and easy to remember.

To RE-Start, **RESTATE.**

In order to get back into the first step of your SELL offense (the Start), simply restate the objection as a question.

Say it again and etch it into your brain.
To RE-Start, **RESTATE.**
To RE-Start, **RESTATE.**

Avoid sounding like a parrot, but you don't need to get real elaborate on what you say to restate. It could be as simple as the following examples:

"Your price is too high!"
RESTATE = "Too high?"

"We are happy with our current supplier."
RESTATE = "Totally happy?"

"Every time I gave you a chance you failed miserably."
RESTATE = "Every time I failed you?"

You can also use generic restates such as "Seriously?" or "Really?" or a favorite down south, "How ya mean?" Just make sure you restate appropriately for the situation at hand—and bite your lip if you are prone to jump in with your answer at this juncture!

Watch your tone and make every effort to transmit a sincere and submissive restatement. Your main objective here is to assure listening and show understanding while getting back into the Start of the SELL Process, and then on to the subsequent steps of your offense.

Restating is a beautiful play that puts you back on offense and back in control with minimal adversity. With one fell swoop you are back on offense and they are on defense, with a natural compulsion to defend *why* they said what they just said. Sure, some spiteful people might say, "Yeah, that's what I said! Pick your ears." Experience, however, confirms that frequently the other person will respond with additional information that may be vital in assessing the direction to take next. Meanwhile, you just created some time to think and regroup! Sometimes restating provides a playback so the other person re-hears what they just blurted, then recants all or part of what they now hear to have been over the edge or unrealistic. Remember, there are so many reasons that might be behind a person's objection. You really do not know what generated the one you are facing. Just RESTATE, and hold steady.

Then, fluidly you are back in your offense on step two, Evaluate. Qualify the objection. Is it legitimate? Is it a ploy? As we already learned, when you engage the customer with skillful questions you uncover facts and specifics. Emotions and feelings can be revealed, allowing you to create a consultative role and connect with the other person. At some point in the probing a voice in your head will probably say, "Wow am I glad I withheld the answer I was *going* to give initially!" When you have a legitimate understanding of the scope of the stated objection, you are ready for step three, and your offense can now be "spot on" and persuasive.

Leverage by providing an answer that persuades using confirmed Benefits. Answers can draw on and reinforce points made in your original offense or you can tap into prepared answers. As an application, before we end this chapter, I will encourage you to develop a Defense Playbook: a collection of SELL Defense response tools which include formidable answers in the Leverage step of each sheet. In a team situation there is notable synergy when proven answers to objections are documented and shared. The best practices of your top performers and veterans will take the entire team to a higher level. There might even be some objections that are so specific and perhaps sensitive in nature, that a stock or management-approved answer is in order. There are just some situations where you can't afford to let company representatives shoot from the hip, or worse yet, shoot their foot. A workable technique that is helpful for some when designing answers is: Feel, Felt, Found. It sounds sort of trite, but in practice it is very effective at guiding the delivery of an answer while keeping a disposition of empathy. Your answer follows this simple pattern with unlimited variations to suit, "I respect how you *feel* . . . others initially *felt* the same way . . . and *found* that doing this was worth the investment." Just take that framework, revise the wording to fit and add persuasive detail (which may even include personal experiences)— and voila, a great answer. Next step.

Lock by trial to confirm resolution or acceptance. Remember, Benefits lead to a positive change in the other person's thinking. Resulting action is logical and in fact, imperative! Don't wonder or leave the issue hanging. Lock to confirm resolution of the specific matter, and if the overall interaction is at the door of your primary objective, proceed to the final Lock!

The SELL Process provides the framework to prepare and execute your offense in dynamic interaction. It also becomes the methodology for preparing, perfecting, and practicing for your defensive encounters. It will work for you! Needless to say, this is not a cure-all or guaranteed turn-around for every objection. In some cases, no matter what is said or done, the verdict is set. You may not be able to fix them all, but you can face them all, skillfully maximizing every situation!

Apply the process

 If you created a list of objections that you face, or if you have identified a few that you anticipate in an upcoming interaction, transpose each one to a SELL Defense sheet, and write out your responses. Remember the importance of writing, that we discussed earlier.

Save your written SELL Process responses to objections. The framework of the SELL sheet ensures a proper methodology while providing consistent structure to create the content. It is advisable to update your responses often, continually making improvements to fine-tune their effectiveness. Some objections might even have multiple variations of responses and different core content in the answers. If you are part of a team, find ways to document and compile everyone's input as you develop your SELL Defense "playbook." Tap into veterans and creative individuals. Capture proven ideas and best practices. Explore variations and new approaches. You can assign one or more to each team member, or work on each objection one by one as a group. Team synergy will allow for significant improvement while enhancing camaraderie and unity. Just think of how advantageous this defensive playbook will be for new hires or transfers from other divisions or departments!

Comfortable under pressure

I would also suggest some intensive practice to sharpen skills. This will help enhance delivery and polish tone and non-verbals. I like to call practice on your SELL Defense "defensive drills." You can do dry runs in the mirror or, if possible, practice responses occasionally with other team members. It seems a bit awkward at first, but get over it and get better. Any training events I conduct usually include video recorded and professionally critiqued role-playing plus a session of defensive drills. I always say, you play like you practice!

I remember my junior year in high school basketball. We were a fairly good team—good shooters, very athletic, and pretty good ball handlers. In our first game of the season the opposing team attacked us with a full-court press after every possession. When under pressure, we panicked. We threw away the ball. As frustration escalated, we started fighting amongst ourselves. After losing so many points in turnovers, we had no chance of recovering, and lost miserably.

Guess what we worked on the next week in practice? Right—how to beat the press.

The coach took us to the locker room chalkboard first and showed us the methodology it would require in order to respond correctly. We then walked through it very slowly. Over and over we went through the motions, picking up speed until we got it down to a science. More practice. More review of the required methodology. By Thursday we seemed ready. Our coach then set up a scrimmage with a nearby squad and commissioned them to "pressure my boys like stink on poop." And they did.

But we did mighty good. However, the memory still haunts me of one point when our coach blew his whistle and yelled, "STOP! Don't anybody move." We froze in our spot on the court. He then dramatically paced over to me with a peeved sigh and growled through pursed lips, "Buttrey . . . why are you *here*?" He shoved my shoulders while he tottered me to the other side of the court . . . "You are supposed to be *here* when the ball is on the weak side." I felt a bit embarrassed—but I would much rather be embarrassed in practice than in front of everyone I know in a game. I would much rather stumble in a selling practice scrimmage than in front of the customer or other person I plan to meet! As expected, we were cool and controlled in Friday's big game. So good at beating the press, we got a few easy lay-ups. The other team's coach ended up changing his strategy and removed the press.

Anticipating scenarios and preparing for them is a worthy discipline. For example, top gun fighter pilots spend considerable time in simulators. Obviously, bomb squads practice disarming procedures using simulation too. Captain "Sully" Sullenberger, a notable advocate of safety preparedness, landed a jet with two bird-struck engines into the Hudson River in 2009 with an uncanny coolness. He had anticipated situations like that and was trained and ready.

I have heard it said that practice makes perfect. Rick Pitino says, "*perfect* practice makes perfect!" Learn the fundamentals. Learn the process. Learn the right moves; then practice the daylights out of them until they become instinctive—automatic.

Vince Lombardi informed us that, "You teach discipline

by doing over and over, by repetition and rote, especially in a game like football *(or I would add selling)* when you have very little time to decide what you are going to do. So what you do is react almost instinctively; naturally. You have done it so many times over and over and over again."

Winners execute fundamentals skillfully . . . by habit.

In our final chapter, I will challenge and inspire you to build on what you ascertained in learning your SELL offense and defense . . . and KEEP GETTING BETTER!

Chapter 8
Keep getting better

Selling is primarily a personally driven, individual sport.

You may be new at selling or perhaps it is familiar territory but either way, improving on the process is up to *you*. There is unlimited potential for personal improvement ahead. This book of the SELL Process provides a suitable foundation for the gamut of skills necessary for effective interaction. For some, this logical framework has even facilitated a reformulation of your selling system. From here you need to have the personal discipline to augment your process with expertise in relationship skills, communication skills, listening skills, style adaptability, strategic acumen, marketing, and more. Plus, in each step of the SELL Process we introduced counsel that must be assimilated purposefully through regular use. I encourage you to go back and reread this book slowly, underlining or highlighting critical segments, meditating on the concepts. Keep in mind that it is all about basics, the fundamentals. Brilliant execution of fundamentals wins.

One summer, a professional basketball player came to a local university in my town offering a four-day training camp. As a starter for my high school team, I signed up. I thought I was pretty good at the game but I wanted to improve. What did we work on? Basics. Each clinic was followed by repetitive drills on the fundamentals. I came quickly to the realization that I was not as good as I thought I was. I was playing with the big dogs, and I was woeful. I had leaned on a few inherent gifts, my eagerness, and maybe just pure adolescent vigor, while my core competencies in the fundamentals were greatly lacking. (Regretfully, this example reflects my early selling days as well!) But something clicked. I left there with a drive to get better. I left there feeling like I hope *you* will feel as you finish this book. I was *challenged by my inadequacy . . . and driven to practice*. I worked the rest of that summer at my driveway hoop running the drills, visualizing the offensive and defensive maneuvers; working the basic skills.

I hope you are challenged by your revealed weak areas and are driven to practice your selling skills!

Practice

Practice in the SELL Process will no doubt result as you utilize the process in a wide array of your daily selling interactions. Mere cognizance of the process will provide an awareness and perspective about where you are in the interaction, triggering improvements and on-your-feet flexibility. This will help, but significant advancement will require a more structured approach. To assure improvement, begin a pattern of post-interaction self-critique. Immediately after each sales call or selling interaction ask yourself, "How did I do?" Mentally review the dialog. Allow yourself, with an open mind, to analyze the effectiveness of what you said and how you said it. Watch the film in your mind and honestly face those key plays where momentum might have changed or opportunities might have presented themselves. Even if it causes you to squint and cringe a bit in embarrassment, swallow the bitter medicine and get better. You may even scan through your written pre-plan and see if you can make specific wording or content improvements for next time. Gather proven Starts, questions, answers to objections, and other nuggets, and document them in your offense and defense playbooks!

And there is more you can and must do. Corrections in the fray or remorseful resolve will only have mild impact on improvement. Practice and rehearsal is the requisite. Any professional athlete, accomplished musician, or battle-ready soldier will attest that perfect, diligent practice is the recipe for maximum achievement. PGA golfers hit hundreds and hundreds of balls per day. Amazing guitar riffs are no accident. In the military, tactical maneuvers are so repetitiously performed, they can be perfectly executed in a moment's notice.

Here are some practical ways to develop good selling "muscle memory":

· Run through your SELL pre-plans in front of a mirror. Practice over and over on critical elements (like Starts or key questions) until they are natural and flow from memory. Visualizing your offense and defense systematically through the SELL Process readies you for success.

· Bounce segments of upcoming interactions off of a coaching manager, colleague, or friend. If you select a person with a similar personality style as your pending contact, it is even more helpful. These types of scrimmages also work really well on the phone. Ask a trusted and respected mentor to play the part of the other person on the phone and then soak up an honest critique when you are done. This is more impactive than you might imagine.

· Repeat your Start over and over, word for word, under your breath as you drive to a meeting or sit in a lobby. Mental rehearsal has been proven to fire the same synapses in the brain as actually performing the activities.

· Watch film. Granted, your selling games are not televised (thank goodness). If they were you would have access to a powerful tool to scrutinize performance and pinpoint shortcomings that necessitate intensive practice. If you have the guts, role-playing is a viable option. I role-play and conduct role-plays as a trainer all the time. Today's technology allows recording on smartphones, laptops, camcorders etc., providing an easy way to play back the practice and see areas that need improvement, firsthand. When you see yourself on video or hear audio recordings of your selling, it rocks your world. Many times habitual blind behaviors are confronted and tackled. Some of you are feeling a puke come on just thinking about this, but give it a chance if you can. Role-playing is never exactly like real life and stage jitters are perfectly normal. Try to look past that. I have witnessed the undeniable value that recorded role-playing provides. Even if it just exposes a few little tendencies or tactical errors, it is worth the pain. There are no "little things" when it comes to dynamic human interaction. In sales professional training camps we religiously role-play a target account situation selected by the individual—the one they applied the SELL Process to in the training. We also typically write custom role-play scenarios ahead of time to construct essential selling situations that demand practice. These are role-played as well, for an intensive practice session. Career professionals realize after the exercise that this workout is non negotiable if someone wants to become a true sales professional.

It takes personal discipline and practice to improve your selling game. Jerry Rice is said to have had the most rigorous workout schedule in the NFL. Talent and good hands are a gift from God, but what it takes to succeed and be a superstar is hard work. The harder you work, the luckier you will get!

The conclusion is this: practice, practice, practice! Just learning the process is not enough. The only way to keep getting better is to apply the process and refine it perpetually.

Now that you have walked through your SELL Offense and have the framework in your head, mastering the process will require consistent usage. I strongly recommend pre-planning with the SELL Process for every sales call or interaction.

In chapter two, I suggested that the SELL Process Planning Tool should be used religiously as a *regimen*. Putting the tool into daily practice as a regimen is, perhaps, the only sure way to develop the high level of selling interaction skill that you desire—or that your job demands.

I am convinced that all significant improvement requires a regimen, which by definition is *a prescribed course of treatment; a way of life*. Regimens allow sustainable improvement without disrupting balance. In fact, adding or changing to the correct regimens will enhance balance!

I used to be athletic, but the demands and pressures of family and business gradually pushed out exercise. Travel and busy schedules gave way to poor eating habits. For fifteen years I made statements like, "I need to lose a few pounds" or "this gut has to go." Yet I followed those with weak comments like, "no matter what I eat, I stay about the same" and "I try to exercise when I can and I always take the stairs, but I can't lose any weight."

Finally, one day I realized that I needed to make some decisive changes. I was feeling low on energy. It was hard to recuperate after big events. Acid reflux plagued me. Medicines covered the real issues. So I found the resolve to begin a regimen. I prescribed consistent new eating and exercise actions. Sure, I still ate some fun food, but I began a daily regimen of walking for thirty minutes every morning and evening. I changed my diet to a much healthier routine.

I was amazed at the steady improvement. After fifteen years of middle-aged sluggishness, now the pounds started dropping off every day! And the best part is that I started feeling better than ever. I had energy and performance like I was twenty years younger. I share this because it was a *regimen* that provided a realistic vehicle to make these improvements happen.

Are your sales sluggish? Are your results with other people waning? It will take a regimen of pre-call planning to build you up to become a sales professional.

I hope this challenge will click something in your core and motivate you to stop making excuses and make some simple, regimented changes. Then keep it up and watch the results happen.

There is a Chinese proverb that says:

"If you want to know your past—look into your present conditions. If you want to know your future—look into your present actions."

Practicing your skill set and developing the personal discipline to choose and stick to proven regimens is a formula for success. The choice is up to you and I hope you make your decision today. Then, don't go it alone. Solicit and receive coaching, accountability, and reinforcement from others.

Reinforcement

This book may be read by a wide audience of individuals that desire to improve in pursuits that involve selling. Many may be selling as a career and be part of a team. Team development involving compelling leadership and coaching provides a culture for exponential personal and corporate growth. Let's devote some attention to current and future sales leaders, managers, and mentors.

Sales professional management can be a daunting challenge and is unique compared to the management of other groups of people. I chose the word "daunting" because leading salespeople can be a bit intimidating. The Latin root of the word daunting means "to tame." I'm sure that most sales managers can relate to that! Sales professionals often have autonomous jobs that require self-motivation and self-discipline. They are out there doing what they do in very dynamic situations—not in a controlled environment. Therefore, the need for compelling leadership, proper structure, standardized tools, and the skills of a winning coach are very helpful. As the leader, you must inspire and direct your team to assure success. The attributes of a compelling leader and the skills required to motivate people is another book in itself. As it relates to the SELL Process, the challenge of sales leaders is to establish and standardize the use of this powerful tool. Expect salespeople to do the discipline of pre-call planning, and facilitate development of their skill in the process! Ferdinand Fornies made it clear, "Management is doing those things necessary to deny those who work for you the unpleasant opportunity of failing."

Organizations that have been introduced to the SELL Process—the ones that capitalized on the breadth of its impact—are the ones who have decided to *standardize* it. Michael E. Gerber in his ingenious book, *The E Myth*, stated, "If you tell people to do the right things and your system tells them otherwise, the system will win every time." *Standard* is a term often used to define a guideline or benchmark. A standard is often a required principle or lofty ideal such as a "standard of excellence" or "gold standard." It implies quality. One of the best pictures of the term *standard* is found in its more classic use as a name for a flag. The United States military commonly refers to the American flag as "the standard." In some epic war movies, before a big battle, there is typically a leader on a horse (probably Mel Gibson) who is riding back and forth in front of the troops with a banner, a flag. What is that leader doing? One manager responded to me after that question, "He's gonna get shot!" That response exemplifies the risk assumed, and the resolve required, for a leader to rally the troops to action. If you want to raise the standard of your sales team to win the brutal battle of today's market, be committed to a standard battle regimen. It is vital as a sales leader to standardize your tactical tool of offense and defense—the SELL Process. A compelling case has been built in this book for the proliferation of this tool and the leader's job will be to sell its effectual use to the troops. In Machiavelli's 15th century writing of *The Art of War* he heralded this edict: "For this reason, it is necessary that a General should be an orator as well as a soldier; for if he does not know how to address himself to the whole army, he will sometimes find it no easy task to mold it to his purposes . . . Many things may prove the ruin of an army, if the General does not frequently harangue his men; for by so doing, he may dispel their fears, inflame their courage, confirm their resolution, point out the snares laid for them, promise them rewards, inform them of danger and of the way to escape it . . ."

Never underestimate the direction and inspiration that can be imparted in your "locker room" or "war room"! Coach Bear Bryant, one of the winningest coaches in college football, stated with confidence, "I know what it takes to win. If I can sell them on what it takes to win, then we are not going to lose too many football games."

One ongoing forum to reinforce the SELL Process is in regular sales meetings. Before we look at some ideas, let me preclude that any sales meetings that you provide should have the proper duration, regularity, content, and purpose. Continually re-evaluate your meetings and adjust based on all surrounding variables in your business. Always do your meetings on purpose and include more than just performance outcomes, assignments, or reprimands. Include the components that impact the outcomes—selling skill development! Here are just a few ideas:

- Have each salesperson select another target account periodically for some formal practice. The entire team or small group could conduct a pre-call planning clinic on their target accounts (similar to what we did through this book). This allows sharing and team support.

- Have salespeople share a testimonial or distribute

copies of SELL Process Pre-call Planning Tools that resulted in successful sales. You may want to use the forms as models. Note: They can be handwritten and even look like notes for a test. This is the idea. Using the forms must be personal and practical. The process forces salespeople to think ahead about the dynamic interaction of the call.

· As a group or by assignment, complete model Pre-call Planning Tools for specific industry or market segments, cold calls to certain types of customers, and possibly models for trade shows. Typing these and distributing them can help standardize your professional interaction with customers and provide a tactical guideline for similar calls. (Note: These are not canned or rote models! We have found that many successful tactical plans are repeatable. Of course, the sales interaction is dynamic and unique each time. The processes must stay in harmony. Still, many Starts, questions, Benefits, Locking techniques, defensive responses to objections, etc. are repeatable in similar selling situations). These models may be incorporated into your software and shared electronically.

· Provide workshops for each step of the SELL Process and build your offense Playbook.

· Conduct workshops to develop standard answers or a resource of optional SELL Defense responses. Compile your defense Playbook filled with proprietary gems.

· Consider scheduling each (or at least certain) salespeople to lead and conduct the skill workshops. Involving mentors and key successful salespeople to lead sales meeting segments or assigned parts, fosters ownership. When people teach, they learn. Granted, the team can tire of hearing just one voice. When a front-line team member reinforces, it proves validity for things you have preached all along. I love how this idea encourages teamwork and mutual respect for each individual's contribution and giftings.

The ideas that you come up with from here on out are limited only by your creativity and organizational constraints. Think out of the box and find effective ways to drive this discipline home. Most coaches yell good advice or catch phrases from the sidelines for months before the clockwork offense and defense kicks in.

"It's not what you teach, it's what you emphasize," according to John Wooden. And clearly he knew how to get wins with his teams.

Now, a word on coaching. To be a winning coach, understand that the dynamics of the SELL Process entail ongoing adjustments and often some outside perspective for your people. This includes rookies and veterans! Coach Tom Landry said, "The secret to winning is constant, consistent management. Coaching is making people do what they don't want, so they can become what they want to be." My coach always made us run the steps. Running up and down the steps of the bleachers was grueling. I hated it—but I was thankful when it came to the last exhausting minutes of a tough, overtime game. Get your team to run the steps of the SELL Process! Here are a few coaching suggestions:

- When you conduct role-play sessions, you and other managers can act as critiquers when recorded role-plays are played back. I have created a critique checklist form of core skills and disciplines, to use during training. A checklist helps in providing a consistent, objective critique. Discuss your critique immediately and give the form to the salesperson to file and refer to. Also keep a copy for you to monitor positive improvements and use as a support in reviews. I have always pondered the fact that when a professional athlete does what they do for a profession, everyone sees them—their team, their friends, their coach. Professional salespeople are primarily only seen in action by the customer. When you get a chance to observe your salespeople in action, take full advantage of it.

- Before a joint coaching call, meet to discuss your role in their call. You want to complement each other and ensure that the customer doesn't feel "practiced on." Also, be careful not to take over and run the call unless you absolutely must. This temptation can sabotage the session and demotivate the salesperson. Review the salesperson's SELL Pre-Call Planning Tool before the call to have an understanding of their tactical plan. You may wish to suggest improvements. For critical calls you may choose to pre-call plan together. Conduct a positive and constructive critique after the call. Do this formal critique immediately if you can. Be gentle, but don't pull any punches. This may be their only career input, exposing behaviors that they may be blind to!

· Meet regularly with each person for some one-on-one evaluation. This can be part of a routine review or performance evaluation, but make it count. Include some tangible expectations, like expecting them to utilize their SELL sheets for every interaction. Setting skill improvement goals for each step of the process can make these coaching sessions better than ever. Perhaps, someday, they will praise you as the sales manager that had the biggest influence on their career.

Keep in mind Rick Pitino's advice, "The key to coaching is not what you do, but the way you do it. The intangibles, the motivational parts of the game are the most important facets of it."

I came across an article in a US Airways magazine some time ago by Bob Wyss called "The Iceman Winneth." It was a stimulating story about a pleasant 73-year-old hockey coach who spoke softly with a faint Quebecois accent. I was shocked when I read that Belisle's high-school teams had won 25 straight state titles in Rhode Island, the longest active championship streak in high-school athletics. Over 27 years, Belisle won 710 games, losing 86 and tying 2, an astounding .868 winning percentage. At the time of the article, 15 of his players had gone on to the National Hockey League, and 56 received college athletic scholarships. Wow. So I scanned the article for his secret. Two revealed aspects of his closed practices included his regimen of disciplines and the fact that "he loves what he does." His son and long-time assistant coach informed us that, "There are no special formulas. His big secret is his ability to teach the basic skills of hockey. He had no fancy plays, he just coached very fundamental hockey."

Practice and reinforcement are essential components of the upward progression of sales professionals. That is what it takes to *keep getting better*. Regular training is foundational to initiate this improvement and assure its sustainability.

Training

Tony Dungy, former coach of the Indianapolis Colts, reminded us, "People that win big games are people that can function in a pressurized environment and do the same things that they do in a training-camp practice . . . "

The obvious importance of seasonal training is modeled in nearly every sport and profession. From doctors to quarterbacks, regular training is imperative and required. It should be no different for those who are in the profession of selling. Success on the field in selling is your livelihood. Training is a time to learn your plays and surface your deficiencies in an intense, undistracted environment. It creates awareness and gets the whole team unified and on the same page. Training is the precondition needed to maximize results and ensure consistent action. Suffice it to say, if you, as an individual, have never had formal sales training or if you, as a leader, have never stopped to provide it for your team—plan it now. If it has been a long time, make the time.

The great Lombardi said, "Truly, I have never known a really successful man who deep in his heart did not understand the grind, the discipline it takes to win."

In addition to training, it is imperative to practice. Support that practice with management reinforcement. Keep getting better. With tenacity you can obtain a small margin of excellence that yields a huge reward.

Consider a major league baseball player that is in a batting slump of .200. What might happen if he keeps that up? Yup, back to the minors. It is cut time. Let's say that guy knows he can do better and spends every day after practice doing additional batting practice. He feels like hitting the showers, but instead he hits a lot of baseballs. He digitally videotapes his swing to catch and tweak minor adjustments on grip, stance, and follow-through. Perhaps he has a coach give him some pointers. As a result, his average climbs to .300. Now what happens? He's a hero who might end up in the Hall of Fame. His pay reflects the performance! Note that the margin of improvement is just *one hit out of 10*. A small margin of excellence yields a huge reward.

What would happen if you got one more *hit* out of 10 in your selling?

Other classic examples include the Olympics. A time edge of .001 might be the difference between a gold medal or oblivion—Nike commercials or no one ever hearing of you again. To get that minuscule margin off of your time, it can take four years of disciplined practice, perhaps a lifetime. Top money winners in the PGA tour often win by a mere stroke or two. And how do you get those strokes off of your game? You hit a lot of balls. Daily. Pit crews carve fractions of seconds from a pit stop by rigid practice, because those tiny moments saved by choreographed perfection win big prizes for the race team. And the same is true in selling interaction.

A small margin of excellence yields a huge reward.

Be aware. That extra level of skill, that minor improvement in the interaction, that slight improvement in tone and non-verbals comes the hardest. You can be *good*. However, to be *great*, you will need to pay the price in training and practice until the SELL Process becomes instinctive—automatic.

You can become a sales professional.

Keep getting better!

This book is only the beginning! Don Buttrey can provide a "Target Account Clinic" on the SELL Process for you and your sales team! In a one-day target account clinic, each person comes to the training with a selected customer account and will prepare for the next, upcoming call with that customer. Participants receive personal help and coaching from Don Buttrey as they learn and apply the SELL Process to real-world selling situations. Workshops and discussion allow insights and help from peers and managers. Securing just a few of the deals worked on by salespeople who attend this clinic can provide an immediate return on investment! These training sessions may also include high-impact role-play sessions—recorded on video and professionally critiqued.

It's time for Sales Training Camp!

Don's primary service is intensive training camps for sales teams. Contact Sales Professional Training, Inc. to discuss your specific needs. Our comprehensive sales curriculum and contact information can be found on our website:
www.salesprofessionaltraining.com

Don is also a proven, powerful keynote speaker for sales meetings and conventions. Make your next meeting one that provides hands-on skills and real help for your team!

You can buy more copies of this book to get it in the hands of everyone in your company that engages in customer selling interactions! Go to:
www.salesprofessionaltraining.com/store
or call: 937-427-1717

Like us on FACEBOOK: Sales Professional Training, Inc.

Follow @DonButtrey on TWITTER
for selling skill tips and inspiration.